COLOR CONTINUUM

NO. 01 MONOCHROMATIC

EMILY CIER

FIVE MODERN MONOCHROMATIC QUILT PROJECTS

Printed in the United States of America

First Printing, 2014

ISBN 978-1499219555

www.CarolinaPatchworks.com

acknowledgments

Sean. For being there.

Maeve. For owls and the color pink.

Liam. For the fabulous patterns you write and the color blue.

Robert Kaufman Fabrics. For providing box after box of glorious Kona Cotton for the quilts.

Angela Walters. For every perfect stitch, swirl, doodle and circle. And Mr. Grumpy Cloud.

The City of Seattle. For being an amazingly beautiful backdrop in all the photographs.

table of contents

introduction 4
sewing basics and tips 5
quilting 8

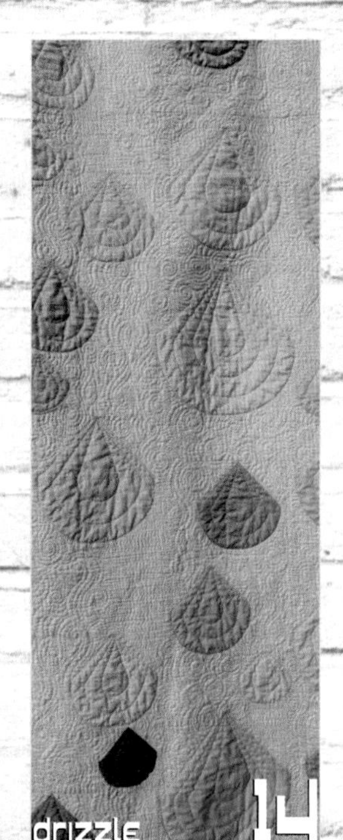

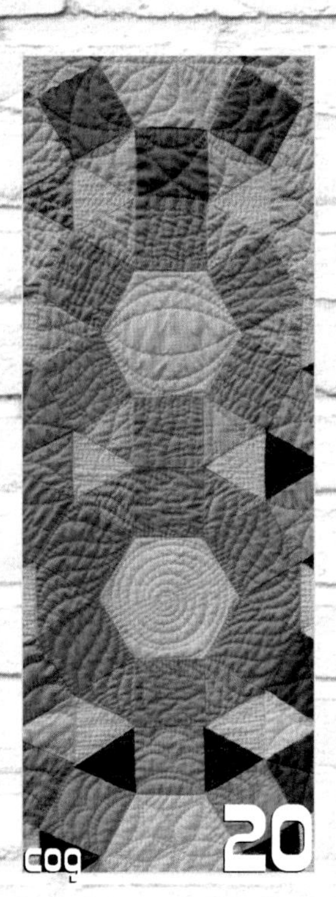

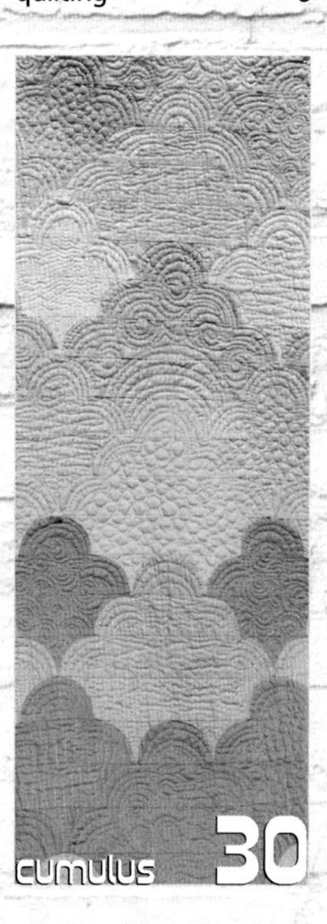

templates 37
resources 43
about the author 46

introduction

Quilts, to me, are about two things: color and shape and how they interact to form a unique and personal creation that we can make, use, and love.

I'm surrounded by the beauty of the Pacific Northwest. The mountains, water and forests that encompass the city of Seattle are the inspiration for the shapes making up these geometric representations of normal day-to-day things.

I often stare out the window as I sew. Watching the ferry boats pass, the colorful sailboats of summer, and storms coming in over the mountains. The colors of the passing days are richly monochromatic — the blues of Puget Sound and summer skies, the warm and glowing sunsets, the fog as thick as syrup, and the rain tapping on the front windows. All while the bustling city of technology and discovery is right on the other side of the hill.

The quilts in color continuum — monochromatic may not all fit the definition of monochromatic you'll find in the dictionary, but are representative of our very all-or-nothing weather patterns — and ever-present scenery — in the place I call home.

sewing basics and tips

All of the projects in this book follow basic, bread-and-butter quilting methods. Here are some basic sewing and quilting tips to help you along the way.

The sample quilts in this book are made with and suggest using Robert Kaufman's Kona Cotton Solids (see *Resources*, p. 43). All of the colors and precut packs were available at the time of the original publication but do sometimes change over time. If you can't find a particular color, find something close and evaluate all the fabrics together before starting your project to make sure they are compatible.

Do I need any special quilting tools?
You won't need any specialty tools beyond your basic quilting supplies. If you are planning on doing a project with templates, you'll need to trace or photocopy the templates (pp. 37-42) for your project.

The following are some basic tools I find handy:

- 24″ × 36″ cutting mat
- Rotary cutter and extra blades: if you can't remember the last time you replaced your blade, it's past time to do so.
- 6½″ × 24″ cutting ruler: my preferred ruler size for long cuts.
- 4½″ square cutting ruler: my preferred ruler size for small cuts.
- Sewing tool basket: always right next to my machine with needles, oil, dusting brush, pins, water soluble pen, etc.

- Robert Kaufman Kona Cotton Solids color card (good to have around and especially helpful for *Oriel*, p. 10 and *Drizzle*, p. 14)

Prewashing: Yay or Nay?

I prefer not to prewash my fabrics because I feel that the small pieces keep their shapes better when they have not been washed, but it's up to you. The fabric yardage requirements given for each project do not factor in shrinkage due to prewashing.

Cutting Notes

- All cuts assume that the fabric is at least 40″ wide.
- The yardage requirements include a small amount of extra fabric in case of a cutting error.
- If you have one, use a 28mm rotary cutter when cutting the concave curve pieces. This smaller blade will make for easier turns.
- When cutting curves, don't cut too many layers at once as you'll end up chopping through the fabrics instead of making a smooth cut. Watch your fingertips and nails!

Piecing Notes

- A ¼″ seam allowance is used for all seams in all of the projects.
- A walking foot isn't just for quilting! It can help keep the feed even when piecing the smallest of seams.
- Make sure not to pull the fabric when pressing, especially around the edges where waves and distortion can occur.
- Mistakes can happen easily in any quilt. Take time to make sure you are using the right color, size, placement, and so on. Don't get frustrated if you end up having to

un-sew a portion at some point. It will be worth it in the end!

- Small sticky notes next to the fabric piles (denoting fabric 'A', 'B', etc) can be helpful in keeping track of which fabric is which, especially when using different colors than are shown in the illustrations.

Quilting and Finishing Notes

- Backing fabric should be at least 4" wider than the quilt top on all sides. Piece your backing fabric if necessary, with a ½" seam pressed open.
- Use your batting of choice, making sure it is at least 4" wider than the quilt top on all sides.
- Make your quilt sandwich by laying the backing wrong side up. Top with batting and then the quilt top right side up, making sure it is centered on the backing and batting. Baste with safety pins about 4" apart.
- Before deciding on a quilting design, check the batting manufacturer's specifications regarding the distance between quilting lines.
- Check out the quilting ideas in photographs throughout this book and pp. 8-9 for ideas and inspiration on quilting these projects. In the last step of each pattern, a *Quilting Idea* note will provide a jumping off point for your quilting design.
- All binding yardage is based on 2½" strips and 40" wide fabric.

quilting

Once you've finished your top, quilting it can be as simple or as intricate as you choose. An all-over stipple or a round of stitching-in-the-ditch will hold things together and still look classy, but I like to think of quilting as an opportunity to have some fun and add another dimension to the project with some whimsical doodles or patterns that reflect and enhance the quilt's overall design.

The talented Angela Walters handled the quilting for all of the projects in this book. Along with each quilt, I sent a small thought as to what I was thinking when it came to the quilting. She took that thought and ran. I've included my thoughts for the quilting in the *Quilting Idea* note at the end of each pattern. Feel free to build on that idea or add your own style to the quilting.

Before you start, make a quilting plan. This needn't be anything formal, it's just a way to get your own thoughts together so that you don't jump in and then change your mind after a few irreversible minutes of stitching. Sketch, doodle, draw on a steamy mirror while getting ready in the morning — whatever works for you.

Check out the pictures above and throughout this book for more examples of the quilting.

For more information on Angela, her quilting, classes and books, I heartily recommend checking out quiltingismytherapy.com.

ORIEL

DIMENSIONS 56″ x 64″
PIECING Emily Cier
QUILTING Angela Walters

Yardage Requirements

Color Melons: Sunrise Charm Squares	four identical 5″ square packs, each pack containing 40 unique colors
Background Melons: Maize-1216	1 yard
Background: Bone-1037	4⅜ yards
Batting	64″ x 72″
Backing: Maize-1216	3⅝ yards
Binding: Salmon-1483	⅝ yard

Additional Supplies

template plastic (optional), 28mm rotary cutter

Step 1: Cutting

1. Iron all fabrics.
2. Trace onto template plastic or photocopy the ***oriel corner*** and ***oriel melon templates*** on p. 38. Trim along the dotted lines.
3. Using the melon template, cut one color melon from each of the 160 5″ squares. Group the cut melons into identical color stacks of four each.
   Note: The Sunrise charm squares pack contains a few extra squares that are not used in this project (Bubble Gum, Maize and Tangerine).

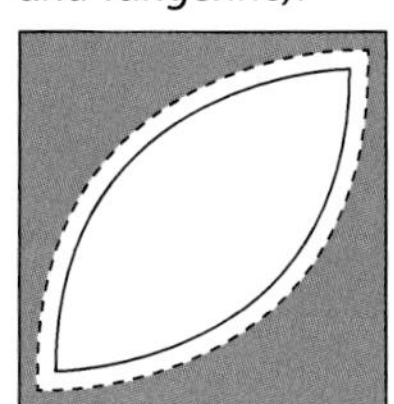

4. Cut the background melons fabric (not the background fabric) into 7 strips measuring 4½″ x WOF (width-of-fabric). Using the melon template, cut 64 background melons.

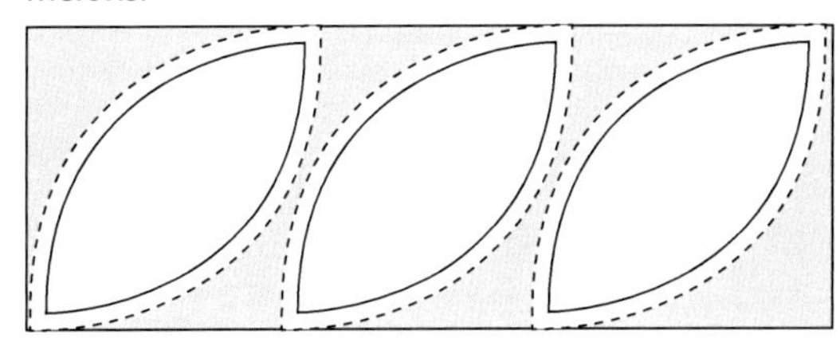

5. Cut the background fabric into 32 strips measuring 4½″ x WOF. Using the corner template, cut 448 corners. Nest this cut to conserve fabric. You should be able to cut 14 corners per WOF strip.

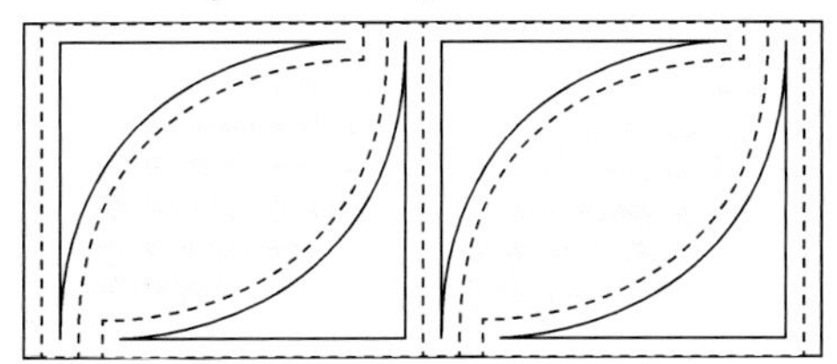

Cutting Notes

- A 28mm rotary cutter can be helpful in cutting the tight curve of the corner template.
- Be careful with the bias edges after cutting the curves. Starching before cutting can help keep the stretching under control.
- Don't try to cut too many layers of fabric at once. A sharp blade will cut accurate and smooth curves.

Step 2: Block Assembly

1. Take one melon and one corner piece. Fold each in half and finger press a crease in the center.
2. Place the two pieces right sides together with the **corner** piece on top. Align the center crease and pin.

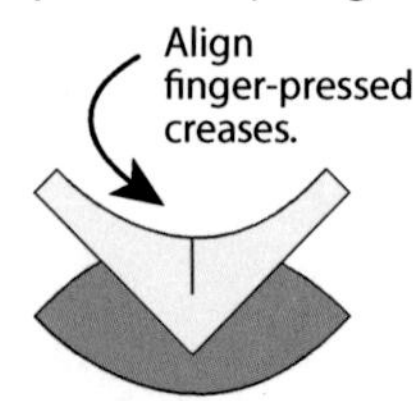

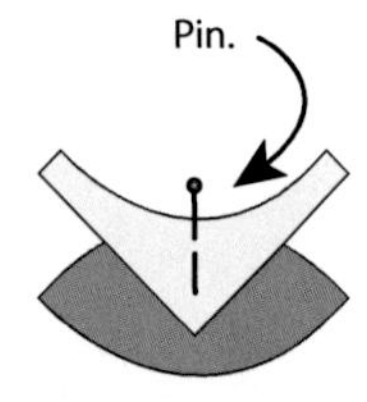

3. Align the curves on the left side and pin. Repeat on the right side.
Note: If you are unfamiliar with sewing curves, you may want to add more pins along the curve to hold the fabric in place while you sew.

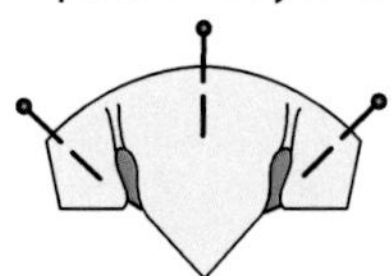

4. Keeping the corner piece on top, sew the curve with a ¼″ seam. Press the seam toward the corner piece.
5. Repeat on the other side of the melon. Press the seam toward the corner piece.

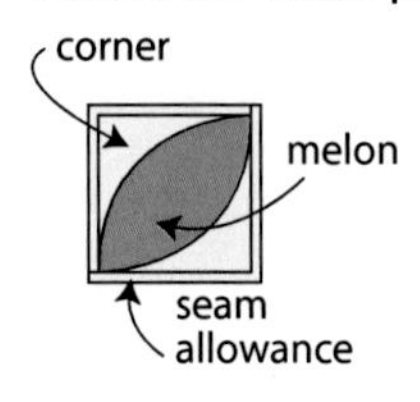

6. Once all four melons of a single color are sewn, sew them into a completed block. Press seams open.

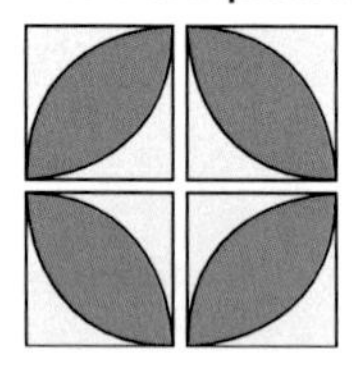
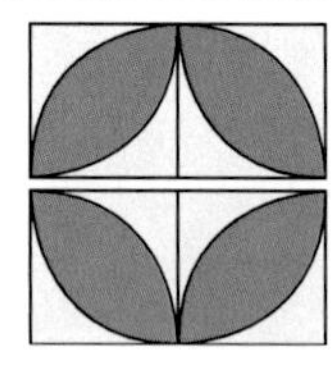
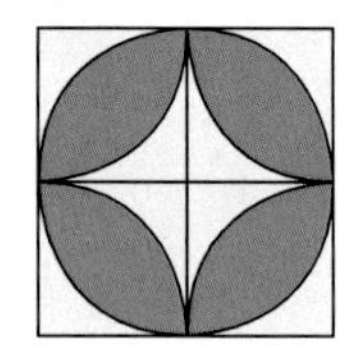

7. Repeat to make the remaining 39 color and 16 background blocks.

Step 3: Quilt Top Assembly

1. Following the **Quilt Assembly Diagram**, sew the blocks into 8 rows. Press seams open to reduce bulk.
Note: The diagram specifies the exact Kona color placement noted within the quilt. If you do not have a color card to identify and match up the colors to the diagram, lay all the squares out to get a general color/light/dark placement similar to the diagram before you begin sewing the rows.
2. Sew the rows together into a completed quilt top. Press seams open to reduce bulk.

Step 4: Quilting and Finishing

1. Cut and piece your backing fabric.
2. Layer your backing, batting and quilt top. Baste.
3. Quilt, trim edges and add binding.

Quilting Idea

- Follow the curves and think of traditional cathedral window patterns.

Quilt Assembly Diagram

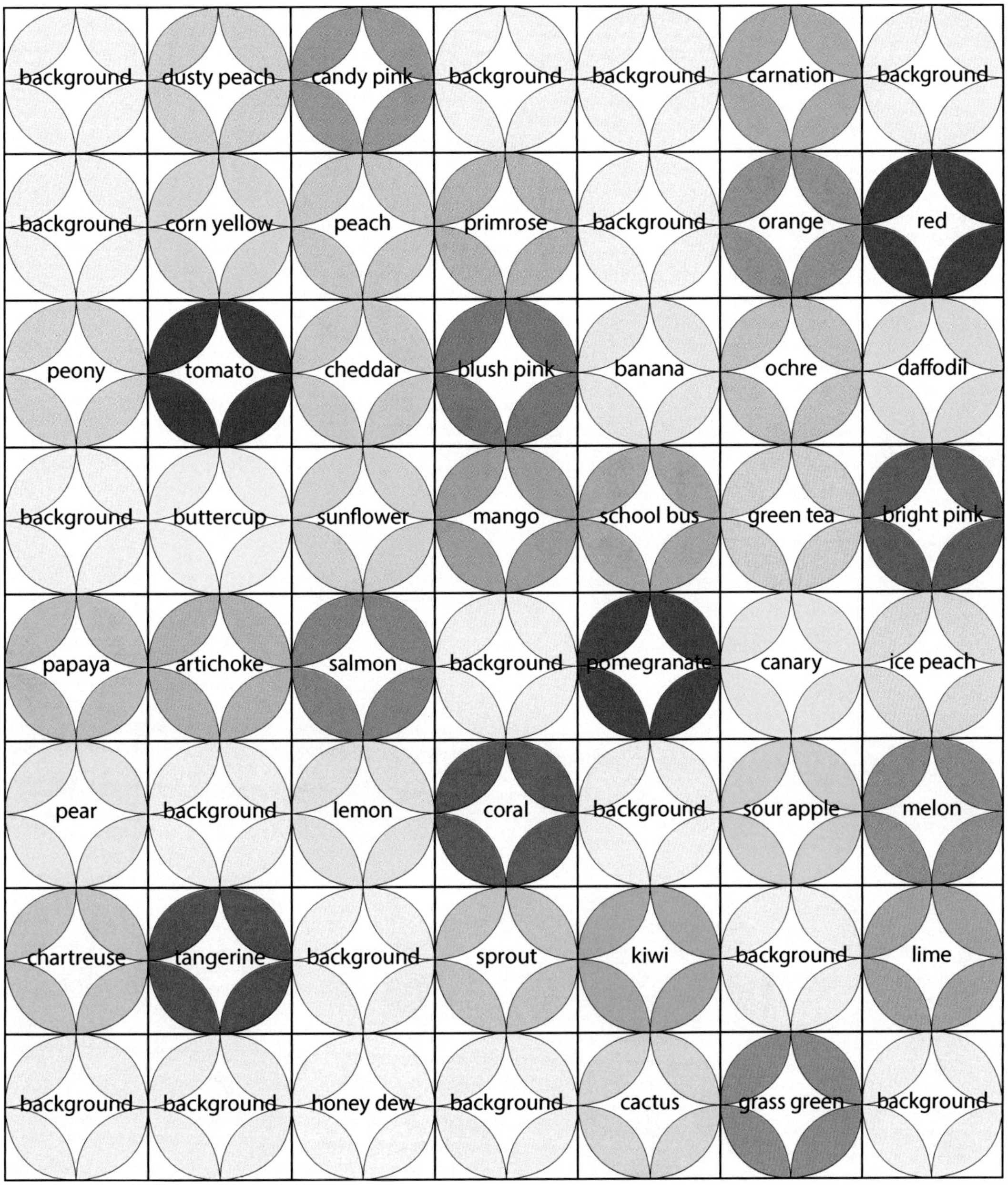

background	dusty peach	candy pink	background	background	carnation	background
background	corn yellow	peach	primrose	background	orange	red
peony	tomato	cheddar	blush pink	banana	ochre	daffodil
background	buttercup	sunflower	mango	school bus	green tea	bright pink
papaya	artichoke	salmon	background	pomegranate	canary	ice peach
pear	background	lemon	coral	background	sour apple	melon
chartreuse	tangerine	background	sprout	kiwi	background	lime
background	background	honey dew	background	cactus	grass green	background

DRIZZLE

DIMENSIONS 70″ x 80″
PIECING Emily Cier
QUILTING Angela Walters

Yardage Requirements

A: Oyster-1268	5½ yards
B: Dusty Blue-362	1 fat quarter
C: Azure-1009	1 fat quarter
D: Aloe-197	1 fat quarter
E: Aqua-1005	1 fat quarter
F: Ice Frappe-1173	1 fat quarter
G: Candy Green-1061	1 fat quarter
H: Robin Egg-1514	1 fat quarter
I: Pond-200	1 fat quarter
J: Sage-1321	1 fat quarter
K: Bahama Blue-1011	1 fat quarter
L: Turquoise-1376	1 fat quarter
M: Lagoon-139	1 fat quarter
N: Cyan-151	1 fat quarter
O: Caribbean-1064	1 fat quarter
P: Jade Green-1183	1 fat quarter
Q: Teal Blue-1373	1 fat quarter
R: Emerald-1135	1 fat quarter
S: Everglade-356	1 fat quarter
Batting	78″ x 88″
Backing: Oyster-1268	5 yards
Binding: Sage-1321	¾ yard

These fat quarters are available in the Grecian Waters *fat quarter bundle from* Robert Kaufman Fabrics.

Additional Supplies

template plastic (optional), 28mm rotary cutter, water soluble pen

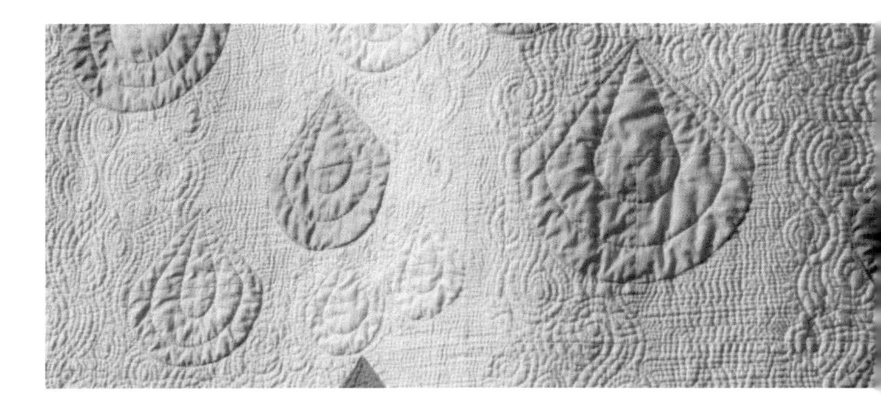

Step 1: Cutting and Assembling Flying Geese

Each of the flying geese is constructed in the same fashion but in different sizes, colors, and quantities. Use the following instructions along with the **Cutting Chart: Flying Geese** to make the size/color combinations needed.

1. Iron all fabrics.
2. Cut the A pieces listed in the **Cutting Chart: Flying Geese** on p. 16. For colors B-S, cut 4½″ x 2½″, 6½″ x 3½″, 8½″ x 4½″ and 10½″ x 5½″ rectangles in the quantities listed in the **Flying Geese Combinations** chart. For each combination, you will need one full rectangle. For example, in the first row of the Combinations chart, for fabric B, cut three 4½″ x 2½″ rectangles, one 6½″ x 3½″ rectangle and one 8½″ x 4½″ rectangle.
3. Draw a line on down the diagonal center of each A square with a water soluble pen.
4. Place one A square at one end of a colored (B-S) rectangle, right sides together.
5. Sew along the line.
6. Trim the excess of both layers, leaving a ¼″ seam.

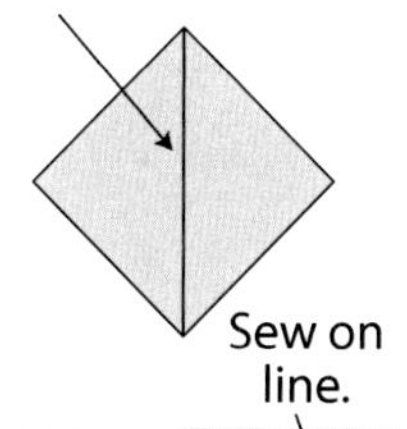

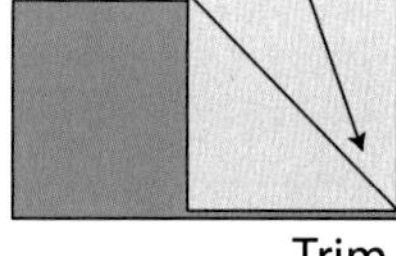

Trim.
Excess to toss.

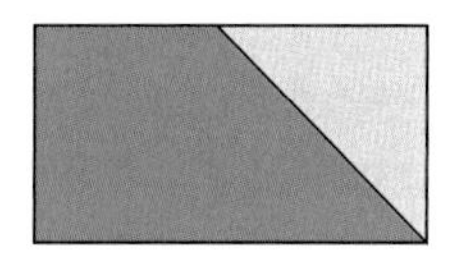

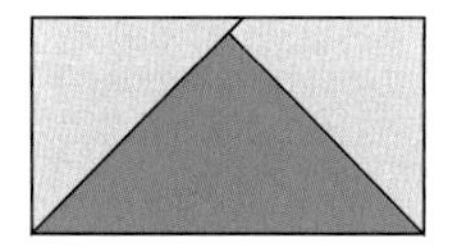

Cutting Chart: Flying Geese				
	First Cut		Second Cut	
	Dimensions	Quantity	Dimensions	Quantity
A	2½" x WOF *	3	2½" x 2½"	48
	3½" x WOF	5	3½" x 3½"	50
	4½" x WOF	3	4½" x 4½"	20
	5½" x WOF	4	5½" x 5½"	24

* WOF=width-of-fabric

For colors B-S, cut 4½" x 2½", 6½" x 3½", 8½" x 4½" and 10½" x 5½" rectangles in the quantities listed in the Combinations chart below. For each combination, you will need one full rectangle.

Flying Geese Combinations				
	4½" x 2½"	6½" x 3½"	8½" x 4½"	10½" x 5½"
A/B	3	1	1	
A/C		1		2
A/D	1	3		
A/E	1	2	1	
A/F	7	1		
A/G	1	2	1	
A/H	1		1	1
A/I	1	2		1
A/J		1	1	1
A/K	1	1	1	1
A/L				2
A/M		2		1
A/N	1	2	1	
A/O	3	3		
A/P	1	1		1
A/Q	1	2		1
A/R	1	1	1	1
A/S	1		2	

7. Press seam to one side.
8. Repeat Steps 3-6 on the other end.
9. Repeat for the remaining colored rectangles.

Step 2: Cutting and Assembling Quarter Curves

1. Iron all fabrics.
2. Trace onto template plastic or photocopy the **2", 3", 4" and 5" inner quarter curve** and **outer quarter curve** templates on pp. 38-41. Trim along the dotted lines.
3. For the background (A: Oyster-1268), cut all four sizes of outer curves using the **outer quarter curve** templates. The quantities for each size are listed in the **Cutting Chart: Quarter Curves** on p. 17.
4. For each color (B-S), cut all four sizes of inner curves using the **inner quarter curve** templates. The quantities for each size are listed in the **Quarter Curves Combinations** chart.

   For each combination listed in the Combinations chart, you will need one inner curve. For example, in the first row, for fabric B, cut six 2½" inner curves (using the 2" inner curve template), two 3½" inner curves (using the 3" inner curve template), two 4½" inner curves (using the 4" inner curve template).

   Note: A 28mm rotary cutter can be helpful in cutting the tight curve of the smaller outer quarter curve templates.

5. Sew the inner and outer curves in the combinations shown in **Quarter Curve Combinations** chart to make the curved pieces.
   a. For each pair of pieces, take one outer curve piece and one inner curve piece. Fold each in half and finger press a crease in each at the spot shown in the diagram.
   b. Place the two pieces right sides together with the outer curve piece on top. Align the center crease and pin.

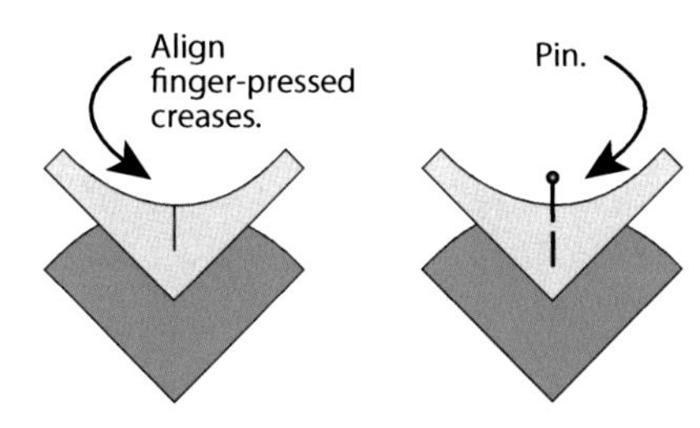

c. Align the corners of the outer and inner curve pieces on the left side and pin. Repeat on the right side.
Note: If you are unfamiliar with sewing curves, you may want to add more pins along the curve to hold the fabric in place while you sew. Even if you don't normally pin your smaller curves, you might find it useful to pin the larger curves.

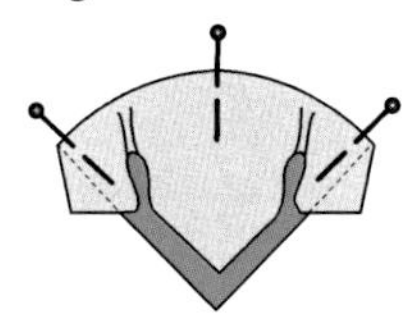

d. Keeping the outer curve piece on top, sew the curve with a ¼" seam. Press the seam towards the outer curve, making sure not to stretch the edges. The block will measure 2½", 3½", 4½" or 5½" square.

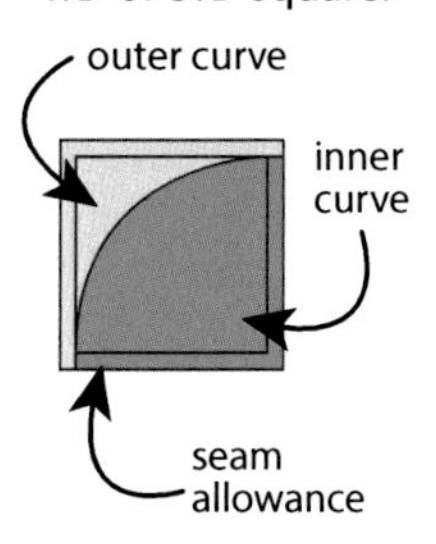

Cutting Chart: Quarter Curves

	First Cut		Second Cut *	
	Dimensions	**Quantity**	**Dimensions**	**Quantity**
A	2½" x WOF	2	2½" template	48
	3½" x WOF	3	3½" template	50
	4½" x WOF	2	4½" template	20
	5½" x WOF	2	5½" template	24

* outer quarter curve templates, pp. 38-41

For colors B-S, cut 2½" (2" template), 3½" (3" template), 4½" (4" template) and 5½" (5" template) inner curves in the quantities listed in the Combinations chart below. For each combination listed, you will need one inner curve.

Quarter Curve Combinations

	2½"	3½"	4½"	5½"
A/B	6	2	2	
A/C		2		4
A/D	2	6		
A/E	2	4	2	
A/F	14	2		
A/G	2	4	2	
A/H	2		2	2
A/I	2	4		2
A/J		2	2	2
A/K	2	2	2	2
A/L				4
A/M		4		2
A/N	2	4	2	
A/O	6	6		
A/P	2	2		2
A/Q	2	4		2
A/R	2	2	2	2
A/S	2		4	

Step 3: Cutting Background

1. Using A: Oyster-1268, cut the number of WOF strips listed under First Cut in the **Cutting Chart: Background**.
2. For the Second Cut, start by taking a strip from the previous step and subcut. Start with the longest subcut, then cut the longest remaining subcut possible from the leftover portion until the strip is too small to be useful.
3. Continue with the remaining strips until all subcuts for that fabric have been made.

Cutting Chart: Background (A: Oyster-1268)

First Cut		Second Cut	
Dimensions	**Quantity**	**Dimensions**	**Quantity**
1½" x WOF	5	4½" x 1½"	4
		6½" x 1½"	7
		7½" x 1½"	3
		8½" x 1½"	6
		10½" x 1½"	5
2½" x WOF	6	4½" x 2½"	7
		8½" x 2½"	7
		10½" x 2½"	13
3½" x WOF	3	6½" x 3½"	4
		7½" x 3½"	3
		10½" x 3½"	5
4½" x WOF	9	3½" x 4½"	6
		4½" x 4½"	3
		5½" x 4½"	4
		6½" x 4½"	24
		10½" x 4½"	10
5½" x WOF	1	10½" x 5½"	1
6½" x WOF	2	10½" x 6½"	6

Step 4: Quilt Top Assembly

1. Construct each 10" block using Background, Flying Geese and Quarter Curve pieces following the **Quilt Assembly Diagram**. Press seams open or to the side as you sew each block. While each block is unique, the basic construction is the same.
   *Note: The smaller 4½" drizzle shapes have a generic assembly explosion in the upper right of the **Quilt Assembly Diagram**.*
2. Sew the blocks into 8 rows.
3. Sew the rows together into a completed quilt top. Press all seams to the side.

Step 5: Quilting and Finishing

1. Cut and piece your backing fabric.
2. Layer your backing, batting and quilt top. Baste.
3. Quilt, trim edges and add binding.

   Quilting Idea

   - Raindrops fall and gather into puddles. Think about vertical lines and ripples in the background and rounded, concentric shapes in the raindrops.

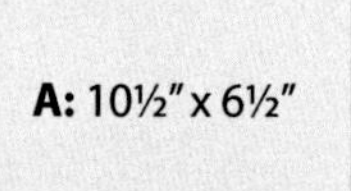

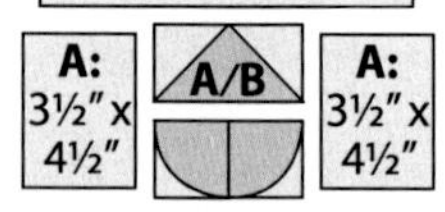

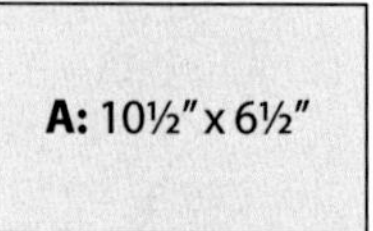

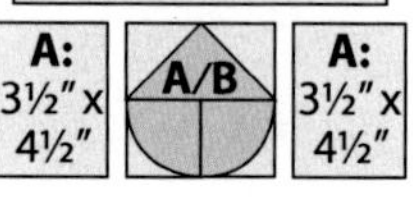

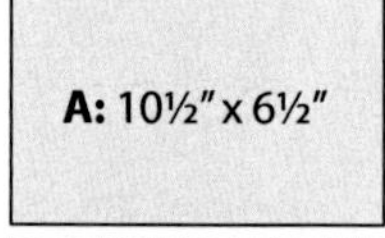

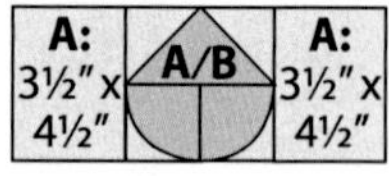

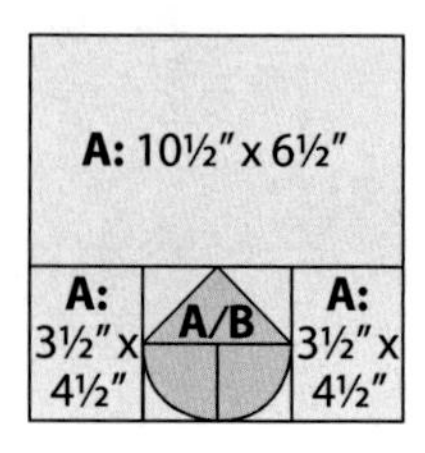

Quilt Assembly Diagram

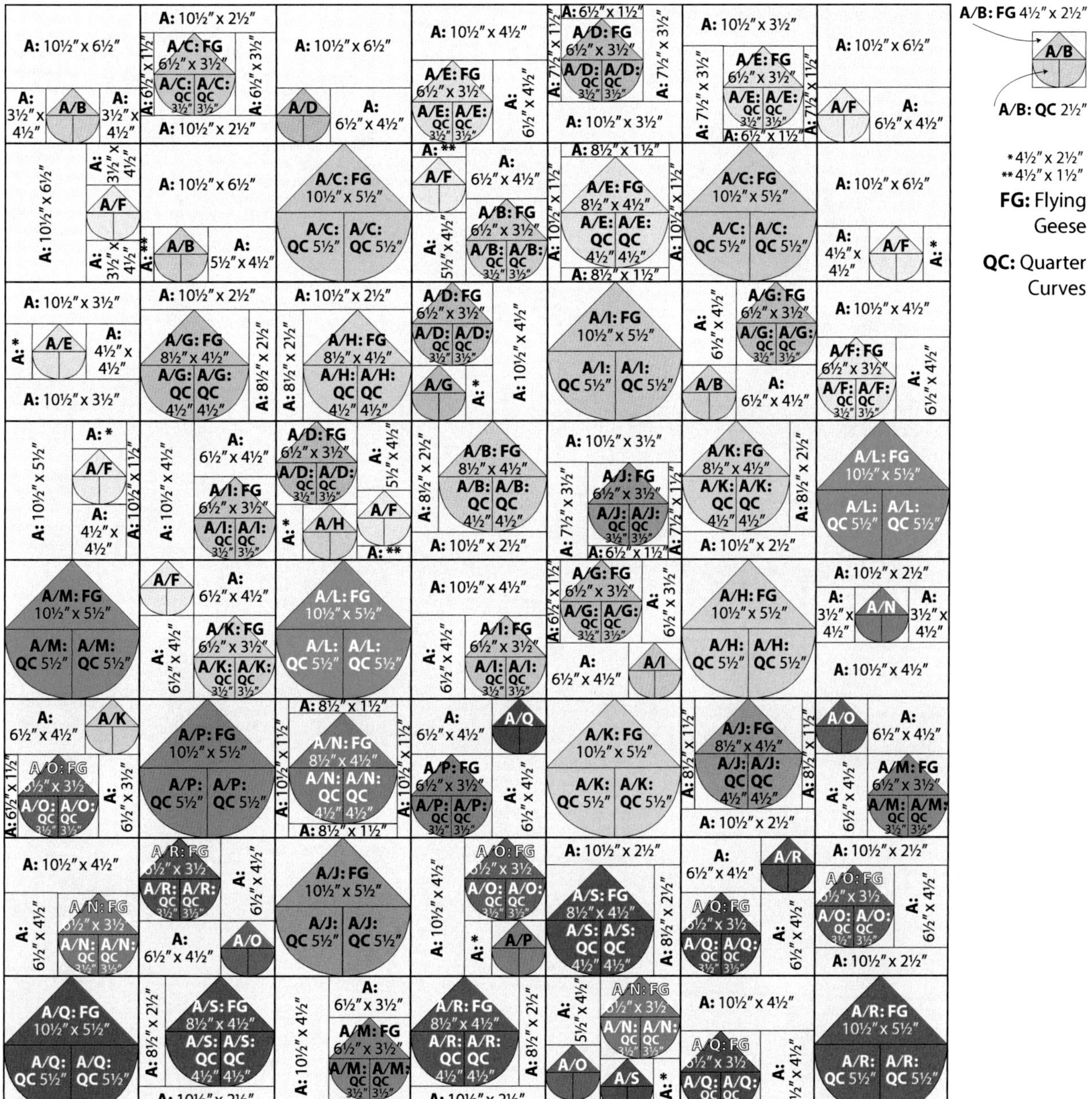

A: 10½" x 6½" · A: 3½" x 4½" · A/B · A: 3½" x 4½"
A: 10½" x 2½" · A: 6½" x 1½" · A/C: FG 6½" x 3½" · A/C: QC 3½" · A/C: QC 3½" · A: 6½" x 3½" · A: 10½" x 2½"
A: 10½" x 6½" · A/D · A: 6½" x 4½"
A: 10½" x 4½" · A/E: FG 6½" x 3½" · A/E: QC 3½" · A/E: QC 3½" · A: 6½" x 4½"
A: 6½" x 1½" · A: 7½" x 1½" · A/D: FG 6½" x 3½" · A/D: QC 3½" · A/D: QC 3½" · A: 7½" x 3½" · A: 10½" x 3½"
A: 10½" x 3½" · A: 7½" x 3½" · A/E: FG 6½" x 3½" · A/E: QC 3½" · A/E: QC 3½" · A: 7½" x 1½" · A: 6½" x 1½"
A: 10½" x 6½" · A/F · A: 6½" x 4½"

A: 10½" x 6½" · A: 3½" x 4½" · A/F · A: 3½" x 4½"
A: 10½" x 6½" · A: ** · A/B · A: 5½" x 4½"
A/C: FG 10½" x 5½" · A/C: QC 5½" · A/C: QC 5½"
A: ** · A/F · A: 6½" x 4½" · A/B: FG 6½" x 3½" · A: 5½" x 4½" · A/B: QC 3½" · A/B: QC 3½"
A: 8½" x 1½" · A: 10½" x 1½" · A/E: FG 8½" x 4½" · A/E: QC 4½" · A/E: QC 4½" · A: 10½" x 1½" · A: 8½" x 1½"
A/C: FG 10½" x 5½" · A/C: QC 5½" · A/C: QC 5½"
A: 10½" x 6½" · A: 4½" x 4½" · A/F · A: *

A: 10½" x 3½" · A: * · A/E · A: 4½" x 4½" · A: 10½" x 3½"
A: 10½" x 2½" · A/G: FG 8½" x 4½" · A/G: QC 4½" · A/G: QC 4½" · A: 8½" x 2½"
A: 10½" x 2½" · A: 8½" x 2½" · A/H: FG 8½" x 4½" · A/H: QC 4½" · A/H: QC 4½"
A/D: FG 6½" x 3½" · A/D: QC 3½" · A/D: QC 3½" · A/G · A: * · A: 10½" x 4½"
A/I: FG 10½" x 5½" · A/I: QC 5½" · A/I: QC 5½"
A: 6½" x 4½" · A/G: FG 6½" x 3½" · A/G: QC 3½" · A/G: QC 3½" · A/B · A: 6½" x 4½"
A: 10½" x 4½" · A/F: FG 6½" x 3½" · A/F: QC 3½" · A/F: QC 3½" · A: 6½" x 4½"

A: 10½" x 5½" · A: * · A/F · A: 4½" x 4½" · A: 10½" x 1½"
A: 10½" x 4½" · A: 6½" x 4½" · A/I: FG 6½" x 3½" · A/I: QC 3½" · A/I: QC 3½"
A/D: FG 6½" x 3½" · A/D: QC 3½" · A/D: QC 3½" · A: 5½" x 4½" · A: * · A/H · A/F · A: **
A: 8½" x 2½" · A/B: FG 8½" x 4½" · A/B: QC 4½" · A/B: QC 4½" · A: 10½" x 2½"
A: 10½" x 3½" · A: 7½" x 3½" · A/J: FG 6½" x 3½" · A/J: QC 3½" · A/J: QC 3½" · A: 6½" x 1½" · A: 7½" x 1½"
A/K: FG 8½" x 4½" · A/K: QC 4½" · A/K: QC 4½" · A: 8½" x 2½" · A: 10½" x 2½"
A/L: FG 10½" x 5½" · A/L: QC 5½" · A/L: QC 5½"

A/M: FG 10½" x 5½" · A/M: QC 5½" · A/M: QC 5½"
A/F · A: 6½" x 4½" · A: 6½" x 4½" · A/K: FG 6½" x 3½" · A/K: QC 3½" · A/K: QC 3½"
A/L: FG 10½" x 5½" · A/L: QC 5½" · A/L: QC 5½"
A: 10½" x 4½" · A: 6½" x 4½" · A/I: FG 6½" x 3½" · A/I: QC 3½" · A/I: QC 3½"
A: 6½" x 1½" · A/G: FG 6½" x 3½" · A/G: QC 3½" · A/G: QC 3½" · A: 6½" x 3½" · A: 6½" x 4½" · A/I
A/H: FG 10½" x 5½" · A/H: QC 5½" · A/H: QC 5½"
A: 10½" x 2½" · A: 3½" x 4½" · A/N · A: 3½" x 4½" · A: 10½" x 4½"

A: 6½" x 4½" · A/K · A: 6½" x 1½" · A/O: FG 6½" x 3½" · A/O: QC 3½" · A/O: QC 3½" · A: 6½" x 3½"
A/P: FG 10½" x 5½" · A/P: QC 5½" · A/P: QC 5½"
A: 8½" x 1½" · A: 10½" x 1½" · A/N: FG 8½" x 4½" · A/N: QC 4½" · A/N: QC 4½" · A: 10½" x 1½" · A: 8½" x 1½"
A: 6½" x 4½" · A/Q · A/P: FG 6½" x 3½" · A/P: QC 3½" · A/P: QC 3½" · A: 6½" x 4½"
A/K: FG 10½" x 5½" · A/K: QC 5½" · A/K: QC 5½"
A: 8½" x 1½" · A/J: FG 8½" x 4½" · A/J: QC 4½" · A/J: QC 4½" · A: 8½" x 1½" · A: 10½" x 2½"
A/O · A: 6½" x 4½" · A: 6½" x 4½" · A/M: FG 6½" x 3½" · A/M: QC 3½" · A/M: QC 3½"

A: 10½" x 4½" · A: 6½" x 4½" · A/N: FG 6½" x 3½" · A/N: QC 3½" · A/N: QC 3½"
A/R: FG 6½" x 3½" · A/R: QC 3½" · A/R: QC 3½" · A: 6½" x 4½" · A: 6½" x 4½" · A/O
A/J: FG 10½" x 5½" · A/J: QC 5½" · A/J: QC 5½"
A: 10½" x 4½" · A/O: FG 6½" x 3½" · A/O: QC 3½" · A/O: QC 3½" · A: * · A/P
A: 10½" x 2½" · A/S: FG 8½" x 4½" · A/S: QC 4½" · A/S: QC 4½" · A: 8½" x 2½"
A: 6½" x 4½" · A/R · A/Q: FG 6½" x 3½" · A/Q: QC 3½" · A/Q: QC 3½" · A: 6½" x 4½"
A: 10½" x 2½" · A/O: FG 6½" x 3½" · A/O: QC 3½" · A/O: QC 3½" · A: 6½" x 4½" · A: 10½" x 2½"

A/Q: FG 10½" x 5½" · A/Q: QC 5½" · A/Q: QC 5½"
A: 8½" x 2½" · A/S: FG 8½" x 4½" · A/S: QC 4½" · A/S: QC 4½" · A: 10½" x 2½"
A: 10½" x 4½" · A: 6½" x 3½" · A/M: FG 6½" x 3½" · A/M: QC 3½" · A/M: QC 3½" · A: 6½" x 1½"
A/R: FG 8½" x 4½" · A/R: QC 4½" · A/R: QC 4½" · A: 8½" x 2½" · A: 10½" x 2½"
A: 5½" x 4½" · A/N: FG 6½" x 3½" · A/N: QC 3½" · A/N: QC 3½" · A/O · A/S · A: * · A: **
A: 10½" x 4½" · A/Q: FG 6½" x 3½" · A/Q: QC 3½" · A/Q: QC 3½" · A: 6½" x 4½"
A/R: FG 10½" x 5½" · A/R: QC 5½" · A/R: QC 5½"

A/B: FG 4½" x 2½"

A/B

A/B: QC 2½"

*4½" x 2½"

**4½" x 1½"

FG: Flying Geese

QC: Quarter Curves

COG

DIMENSIONS 74″ x 75″
PIECING Emily Cier
QUILTING Angela Walters

Yardage Requirements

Snow-1339	2⅞ yards
White-1387	¾ yard
Robin Egg-1514	⅓ yard
Evening-195	⅓ yard
Breakers-440	¼ yard
Stratosphere-448	¼ yard
Pool-45	⅓ yard
Alegria-405	¼ yard
Oasis-446	⅓ yard
Putty-1303	¾ yard
Oyster-1268	¾ yard
Ash-1007	½ yard
Ice Frappe-1173	¼ yard
Aqua-1005	¼ yard
Capri-442	¼ yard
Fog-444	¼ yard
Celestial-233	¼ yard
Azure-1009	¼ yard
Honey Dew-21	¼ yard
Bone-1037	¼ yard
Natural-1242	¼ yard
Batting	82″ x 83″
Backing: Shadow-457	4¾ yards *
Binding: Celestial-233	¾ yard

* You may need additional backing fabric if your fabric is less than 44″ wide.

Additional Supplies

template plastic (optional)

Step 1: Cutting

1. Iron all fabrics.
2. Trace onto template plastic or photocopy the six ***cog (i/O, iii, M/N, P, Q, R) templates*** on pp. 40-42. Trim along the dotted lines (solid lines on M/N template).
3. Cut all of the fabric following the **Cutting Chart** on p. 23. Cuts for M, N, R/P and ii have more detailed instructions in the **Cutting Chart**. Use sticky notes to label the cut fabrics with the color name and piece letter as you go to stay organized.
   Note: Be careful with the bias edges after cutting the angled pieces. Starching before cutting can help keep the stretching under control. Nest all angled cuts when possible.

Step 2: Cog Assembly

While each cog has different colored parts, the assembly for each is the same. Use the **Cog Chart** for the quantities and combinations of each cog to sew.

1. Referring to the Cog Chart, start with Cog A. The center (i) is Snow-1339, the outer ring squares (ii) are Robin Egg-1514 and the outer ring triangles (iii) are Ice Frappe-1173.

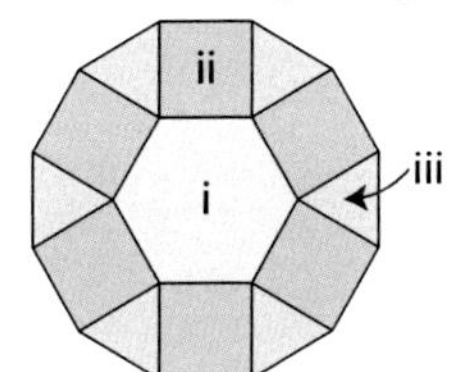

Cog Chart

Cog	i	ii	iii	quantity
A	Snow-1339	Robin Egg-1514	Ice Frappe-1173	6
B	Snow-1339	Evening-195	Aqua-1005	6
C	Snow-1339	Breakers-440	Capri-442	4
D	Snow-1339	Stratosphere-448	Fog-444	3
E	Snow-1339	Pool-45	Celestial-233	5
F	Snow-1339	Alegria-405	Azure-1009	2
G	Snow-1339	Oasis-446	Honey Dew-21	5
H	Snow-1339	Putty-1303	Oyster-1268	5
I	Snow-1339	Oyster-1268	Putty-1303	6
J	Snow-1339	Ash-1007	Bone-1037	5
K	Snow-1339	Oyster-1268	Ash-1007	4
L	Snow-1339	Putty-1303	Natural-1242	8

Gather your fabric pieces and sew one triangle (iii) to the left side of one square (ii). Start and stop your seam ¼" from each end. You MUST do this to be able to complete the inset seams in the following steps.

Repeat with the remaining triangles and squares. Sew two ii/iii units together. Repeat with the remaining ii/iii units. Sew all three units from the previous step and sew together to form the entire outer ring.

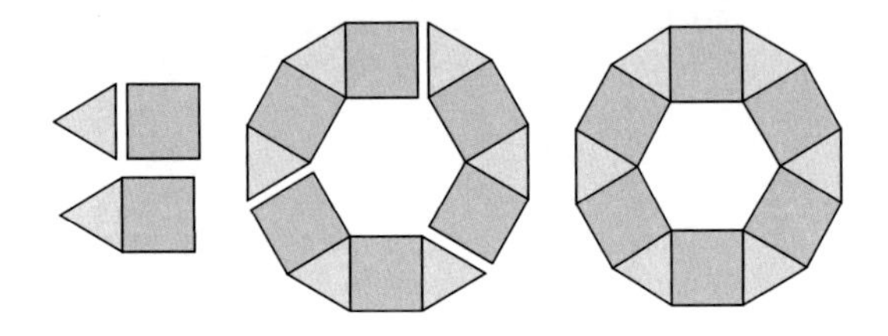

Y-seam Tips:
- Do not press seams open or to the side.
- Many machines have a ¼" quilting foot with markings ¼" on either side of the needle position. If your foot has these markings, they will help immensely here.
- Do not sew over any previously sewn seams.
- Keep your machine in needle-up-when-you-stop-sewing mode.
- If your machine has a knee lift, use it!

2. Take the center hexagon (i) and place the outer ring on top, aligning one seam and with right sides together. Sew the seam, making sure to start and stop your seam ¼" from each end. DO NOT press seams. Working clockwise around the center hexagon, realign the next square in the outer ring so it lines up with the next side of the hexagon and sew. Continue until all squares in the outer ring are sewn to the center hexagon. Do NOT press any seams open or to the side.

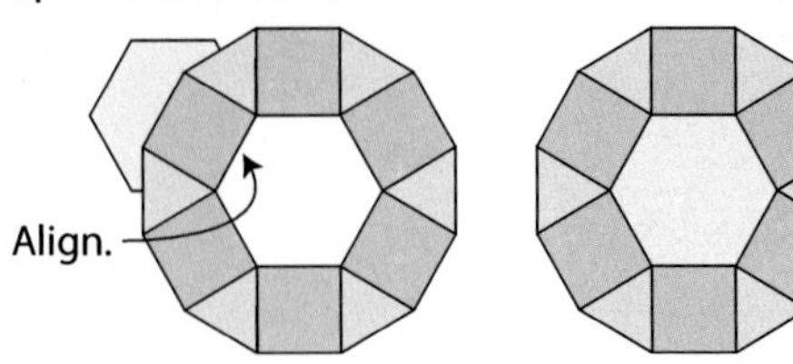

3. Repeat to make the remainder of the cogs in the **Cog Chart**.

Cutting Chart

	First Cut		Second Cut	
	Dimensions	**Quantity**	**Template**	**Quantity**
Snow-1339	4 7/8″ x WOF[1]	9	i	59
	9 7/8″ x WOF	4	M[2]	9
			N[3]	8
	1 3/4″ x WOF	4	Q	14
			R[4]	4
White-1387	2 15/16″ x WOF	7	O	134
			P[4]	20
Robin Egg-1514	3″ x WOF	3	ii (3″ x 3″)[5]	36
Evening-195	3″ x WOF	3	ii (3″ x 3″)[5]	36
Breakers- 440	3″ x WOF	2	ii (3″ x 3″)[5]	24
Stratosphere- 448	3″ x WOF	2	ii (3″ x 3″)[5]	18
Pool-45	3″ x WOF	3	ii (3″ x 3″)[5]	30
Alegria-405	3″ x WOF	1	ii (3″ x 3″)[5]	12
Oasis-446	3″ x WOF	3	ii (3″ x 3″)[5]	30
Putty-1303	3″ x WOF	6	ii (3″ x 3″)[5]	78
	2 15/16″ x WOF	2	iii	36
Oyster-1268	3″ x WOF	5	ii (3″ x 3″)[5]	60
	2 15/16″ x WOF	2	iii	30
Ash-1007	3″ x WOF	3	ii (3″ x 3″)[5]	30
	2 15/16″ x WOF	1	iii	24
Ice Frappe- 1173	2 15/16″ x WOF	2	iii	36
Aqua-1005	2 15/16″ x WOF	2	iii	36
Capri-442	2 15/16″ x WOF	1	iii	24
Fog-444	2 15/16″ x WOF	1	iii	18
Celestial- 233	2 15/16″ x WOF	2	iii	30
Azure-1009	2 15/16″ x WOF	1	iii	12
Honey Dew-21	2 15/16″ x WOF	2	iii	30
Bone-1037	2 15/16″ x WOF	2	iii	30
Natural- 1242	2 15/16″ x WOF	2	iii	48

[1] WOF = width-of-fabric

[2] For M: Subcut the 9 7/8″ x WOF strips into 9 7/8″ x 9 7/8″ squares. Using the M/N Template, trim all four corners to yield a dodecagon.

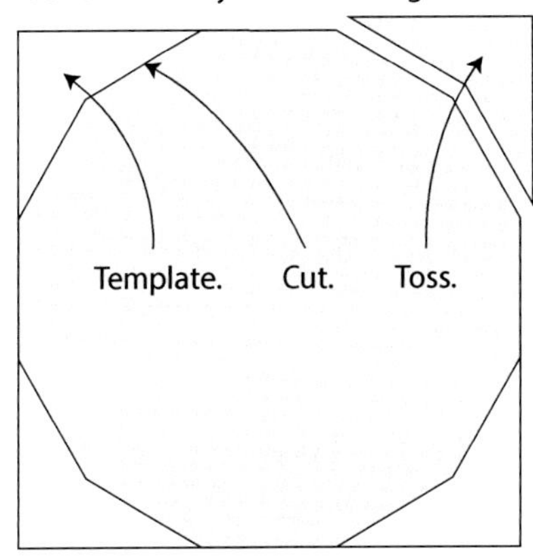

[3] For N: Subcut the 9 7/8″ x WOF strips into 9 7/8″ x 5 1/8″ rectangles. Using the M/N Template, trim two corners along the long edge of the rectangle to yield a half dodecagon.

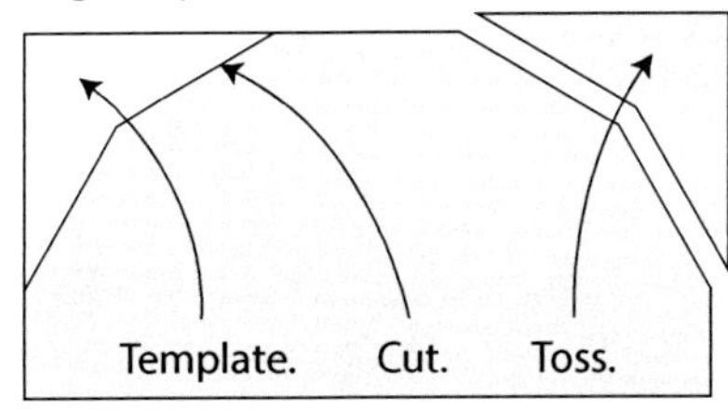

[4] If you are using fabric with right and wrong sides, make sure half are R/P and half are the reverse of R/P. If you are using a solid (where there is no difference in the sides), cut the amount shown in the chart.

[5] There is no template for ii. Subcut all the 3″ x WOF strips into 3″ x 3″ squares.

Step 3: Column and Quilt Top Assembly

All the cogs come together now with the addition of setting pieces M-R.

1. Following the **Quilt Assembly Diagram**, sew the cogs and blank cogs (M and N) into columns by starting with the first two in the column. Place them right sides together and sew a ¼" seam. **Make sure to start and stop your seam ¼" from each end.** DO NOT press the seams open or to the side.
2. Continue adding cogs to the column until it is complete. Add triangles (O and P) in between, on top, and on bottom of the cogs. Number the column with a scrap piece of paper and a pin and set to the side.
3. Continue sewing until all the columns are complete.
4. Place the first two columns on your workspace and align the tops. Flip the right column on top of the left column.
5. Take the first seam and move to your sewing machine. Start with the first seam (**1** in the illustration to the right). Align the seam and sew a ¼" seam making sure you start and stop ¼" from each end. DO NOT press the seam.
6. Align the next section (**2**) and repeat. And repeat and repeat, stopping after each segment to realign. Remember to stop and start ¼" from each fabric edge in each segment.

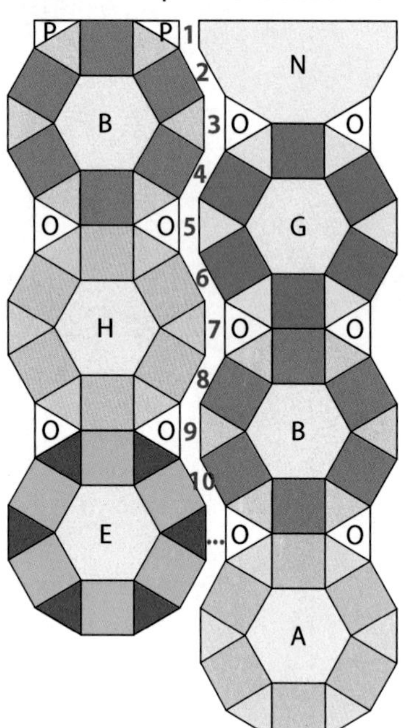

7. Repeat for the remainder of the columns to form the quilt top.
8. Sew the edge pieces (R and Q) into their spots following the same methods used in the rest of the quilt top.
9. Press all seams open to reduce bulk.
   Note: This is a monumental undertaking as nothing can be ironed until all the seams are sewn. Don't get too overwhelmed. You're almost done!

Step 4: Quilting and Finishing

1. Cut and piece your backing fabric.
2. Layer your backing, batting and quilt top. Baste.
3. Quilt, trim edges and add binding.

Quilting Idea

- This is a quilt built on cogs and geometry. Think about angles, gears and linear shapes when quilting this one.

Quilt Assembly Diagram

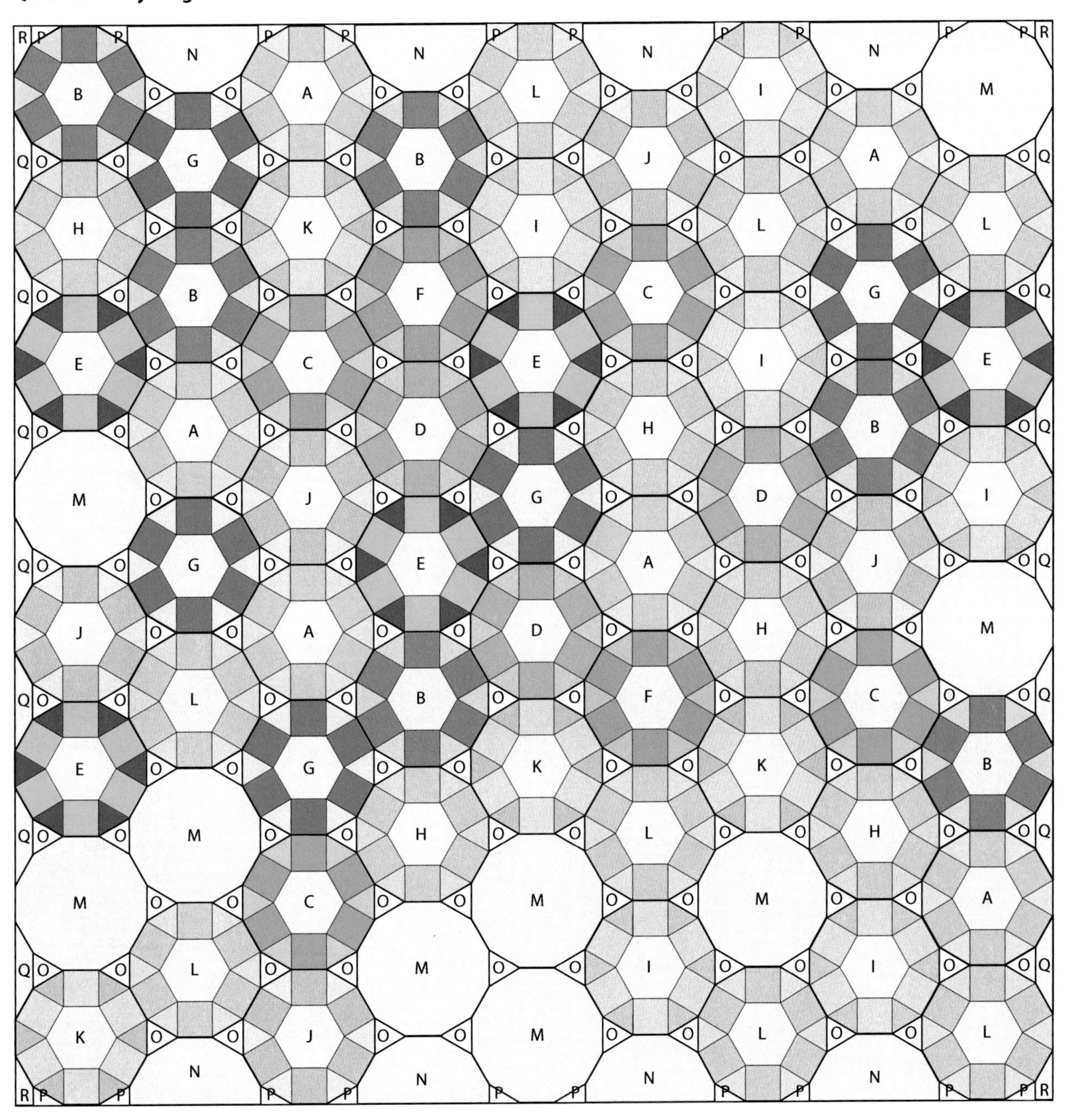

QUILL

DIMENSIONS 69" x 75"
PIECING Emily Cier
QUILTING Angela Walters

Yardage Requirements

A: Oyster-1268	⅜ yard
B: Putty-1303	½ yard
C: Parchment-413	⅝ yard
D: Mushroom-1239	⅝ yard
E: Bison-1017	⅜ yard
F: White-1387	4⅜ yards
Batting	77" x 83"
Backing: Putty-1303	4⅝ yards
Binding: Bison-1017	¾ yard

Additional Supplies

water soluble pen

Step 1: Cutting Background

1. Using F: White-1387, cut the number of width-of-fabric (WOF) strips listed in the First Cut of the **Cutting Chart: Background**.
2. For the Second Cut, start by taking a strip from the previous step and subcut. Start with the longest subcut, then cut the longest remaining subcut possible from the leftover portion until the strip is too small to be useful.
3. Continue with the remaining strips until all the subcuts have been made.

   Cutting Note

   - The cutting chart includes one extra strip and the yardage requirements include a couple extra strips in case of a cutting error.

Cutting Chart: Background

First Cut	
3½" x WOF	26
Second Cut	
33½" x 3½"	5
30½" x 3½"	2
27½" x 3½"	2
24½" x 3½"	4
21½" x 3½"	2
18½" x 3½"	6
15½" x 3½"	2
12½" x 3½"	22
9½" x 3½"	5
6½" x 3½"	8
3½" x 3½"	4

Step 2: Cutting and Assembling Half-Square Triangles (HST)

1. For each fabric, cut the number of 3⅞" x WOF strips listed in the First Cut of the **Cutting Chart: Half-Square Triangles**.
2. For the Second Cut, subcut the strips from the previous step into 3⅞" x 3⅞" squares following the quantities listed in the chart.
3. Combine the fabrics in the combinations shown in the Combinations section and make into HSTs.
   a. Take one Piece 1 square and one Piece 2 square. Stack one on top of the other, right sides together. Draw a diagonal line with a water soluble fabric marker on the wrong side of the top square.
   b. Sew a ¼" seam on either side of the line drawn in (a).
   c. Cut along the center line. Press seams open. Trim triangle tails. You'll end up with two combined squares.
   Note: The combinations will yield twice as many HSTs. For example, 2 A squares (Piece 1) plus 2 F squares (Piece 2) will yield 4 A/F HSTs. You will end up with a leftover from A, C and D.

Cutting Chart: Half-Square Triangles

Fabric	A: Oyster-1268	B: Putty-1303	C: Parchment-413	D: Mushroom-1239	E: Bison-1017	F: White-1387
First Cut						
# of rows	2	3	4	4	2	14
Second Cut						
# of squares	18	26	40	31	20	135
Combinations						
		Piece 1				
		A	**B**	**C**	**D**	**E**
Piece 2	**F**	18	26	40	31	20

Step 3: Strip Assembly

Chain piecing is the simplest way to sew the strips.
Note: All the HSTs are split with F, therefore only the letter of the color fabric (A-E) is noted on the ***Quilt Assembly Diagram****.*

1. Following the **Quilt Assembly Diagram**, sew Piece 1 to Piece 2, Piece 3 to Piece 4, Piece 5 to Piece 6, etc.
   Note: Cut sizes are shown in the diagram. Double check the rotation of each HST before sewing.

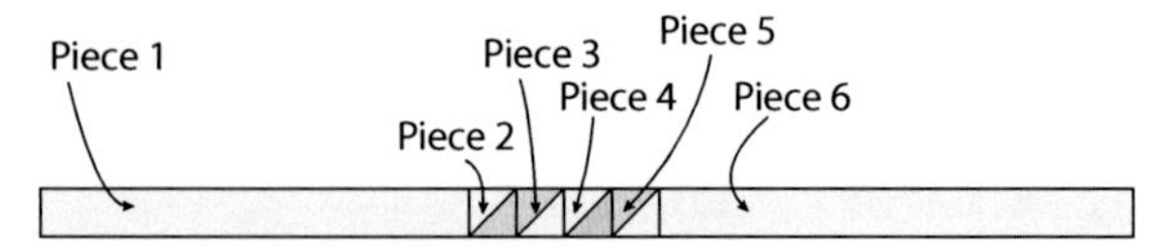

2. Snip the thread in between each unit.
3. Continue chain piecing by sewing unit 1/2 to unit 3/4, unit 5/6 to unit 7/8 (in strips where there are more units), etc.
4. Snip and continue to sew units together until you've completed the entire strip.
5. Set the strip aside until all the strips for that section are complete and then continue with **Step 4: Quilt Top Assembly**.

Step 4: Quilt Top Assembly

1. When all the strips are complete, sew the strips together to form the quilt top.
2. Press seams to one side.

Step 5: Quilting and Finishing

1. Cut and piece your backing fabric.
2. Layer your backing, batting and quilt top. Baste.
3. Quilt, trim edges and add binding.

   Quilting Idea

   - Quill has lots of movement and linear shapes taking you in all directions. Extend these lines with your quilting.

Quilt Assembly Diagram

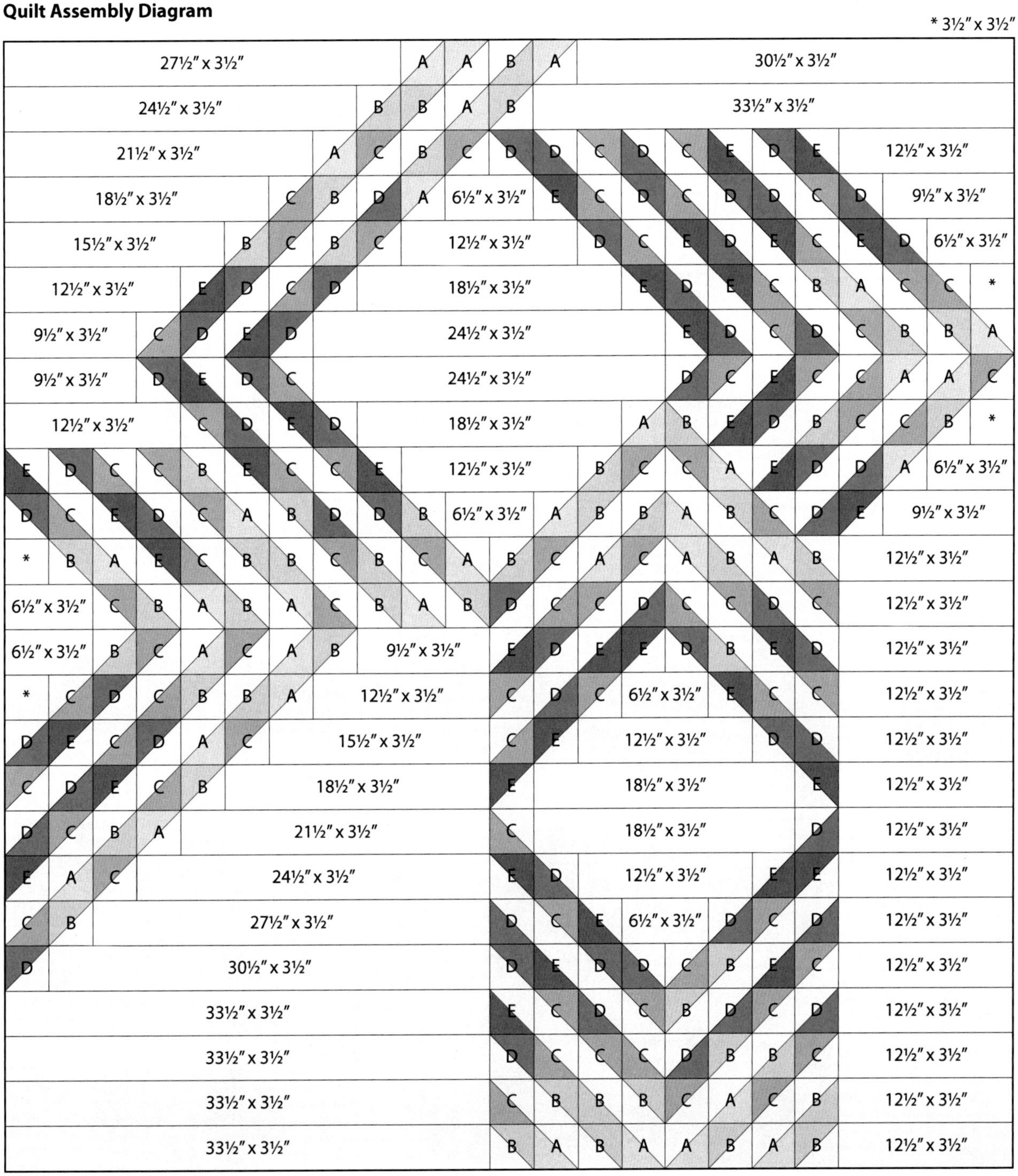

* 3½″ x 3½″

27½″ x 3½″ A A B A 30½″ x 3½″
24½″ x 3½″ B B A B 33½″ x 3½″
21½″ x 3½″ A C B C D D C D C E D E 12½″ x 3½″
18½″ x 3½″ C B D A 6½″ x 3½″ E C D C D D C D 9½″ x 3½″
15½″ x 3½″ B C B C 12½″ x 3½″ D C E D E C E D 6½″ x 3½″
12½″ x 3½″ E D C D 18½″ x 3½″ E D E C B A C C *
9½″ x 3½″ C D E D 24½″ x 3½″ E D C D C B B A
9½″ x 3½″ D E D C 24½″ x 3½″ D C E C C A A C
12½″ x 3½″ C D E D 18½″ x 3½″ A B E D B C C B *
E D C C B E C C E 12½″ x 3½″ B C C A E D D A 6½″ x 3½″
D C E D C A B D D B 6½″ x 3½″ A B B A B C D E 9½″ x 3½″
* B A E C B B C B C A B C A C A B A B 12½″ x 3½″
6½″ x 3½″ C B A B A C B A B D C C D C C D C 12½″ x 3½″
6½″ x 3½″ B C A C A B 9½″ x 3½″ E D E E D B E D 12½″ x 3½″
* C D C B B A 12½″ x 3½″ C D C 6½″ x 3½″ E C C 12½″ x 3½″
D E C D A C 15½″ x 3½″ C E 12½″ x 3½″ D D 12½″ x 3½″
C D E C B 18½″ x 3½″ E 18½″ x 3½″ E 12½″ x 3½″
D C B A 21½″ x 3½″ C 18½″ x 3½″ D 12½″ x 3½″
E A C 24½″ x 3½″ E D 12½″ x 3½″ E E 12½″ x 3½″
C B 27½″ x 3½″ D C E 6½″ x 3½″ D C D 12½″ x 3½″
D 30½″ x 3½″ D E D D C B E C 12½″ x 3½″
33½″ x 3½″ E C D C B D C D 12½″ x 3½″
33½″ x 3½″ D C C C D B B C 12½″ x 3½″
33½″ x 3½″ C B B B C A C B 12½″ x 3½″
33½″ x 3½″ B A B A A B A B 12½″ x 3½″

CUMULUS

Yardage Requirements

Fabric	Crib 44″ x 48″	Throw 60″ x 64″	Twin 72″ x 96″	Queen 96″ x 96″	King 108″ x 96″
A: White-1387			½ yard	½ yard	¾ yard
B: Silver-1333			½ yard	⅝ yard	¾ yard
C: Blue-1028			⅞ yard	1 yard	1 yard
D: Shadow-457			½ yard	⅝ yard	¾ yard
E: Cloud-152		½ yard	⅞ yard	1 yard	1 yard
F: Baby Blue-1010		½ yard	½ yard	⅝ yard	¾ yard
G: Ash-1007	⅜ yard	⅝ yard	⅞ yard	1 yard	1 yard
H: Fog-444	⅜ yard	½ yard	½ yard	⅝ yard	¾ yard
I: Capri-442	½ yard	⅝ yard	⅞ yard	1 yard	1 yard
J: Medium Grey-1223	⅜ yard	½ yard	½ yard	⅝ yard	¾ yard
K: Iron-408	½ yard	⅝ yard	⅞ yard	1 yard	1 yard
L: Pewter-1470	⅜ yard	½ yard	½ yard	⅝ yard	¾ yard
M: Smoke-1713	½ yard	⅝ yard	⅞ yard	1 yard	1 yard
N: Stratosphere-448	⅜ yard	½ yard	½ yard	⅝ yard	¾ yard
O: Shale-456	½ yard	⅝ yard	⅞ yard	1 yard	1 yard
P: Oasis-446	⅜ yard	½ yard	½ yard	⅝ yard	¾ yard
Q: Graphite-295	½ yard	⅝ yard	⅞ yard	1 yard	1 yard
R: Slate-1336	⅜ yard	½ yard	½ yard	⅝ yard	¾ yard
S: Steel-91	½ yard	⅝ yard	⅞ yard	1 yard	1 yard
T: Celestial-233		½ yard	½ yard	⅝ yard	¾ yard
U: Coal-1080		½ yard	⅞ yard	1 yard	1 yard
V: Prussian-454			½ yard	⅝ yard	¾ yard
W: Storm-458			⅞ yard	1 yard	1 yard
X: Charcoal-1071			½ yard	⅝ yard	¾ yard
Y: Pepper-359			⅝ yard	⅝ yard	¾ yard
Batting	52″ x 56″	68″ x 72″	80″ x 104″	104″ x 104″	116″ x 108″
Backing: Celestial-233	3 yards	4 yards	5⅞ yards	8¾ yards	9 yards
Binding: Storm-458	½ yard	⅝ yard	¾ yard	⅞ yard	⅞ yard

Additional Supplies

template plastic (optional), 28mm rotary cutter

Step 1: Cutting Rectangles and Squares

1. Iron all fabrics.
2. For each color, cut the number of 2½" x width-of-fabric (WOF) strips listed in the **Cutting Chart: Rectangles and Squares**.
3. For the Second Cut, start by taking a strip from the previous step and subcut. Start with the longest subcut, then cut the longest remaining subcut possible from the leftover portion until the strip is too small to be useful.
4. Continue with the remaining strips until all subcuts for that fabric have been made.
5. Repeat with the remaining colors.
6. As you cut each color, make a color key for yourself. With this many different blues and greys, mix-ups happen easily. Take a small scrap about 1" x 1" and tape it to a piece of paper, noting its letter next to it.

Cutting Notes

- All cuts assume the fabric is at least 40" wide.
- If you have the table space, you may want to cut your strips for Step 1 and Step 2 at the same time.
- The yardage requirements include a couple extra strips in case of a cutting error.

Step 2: Cutting and Assembling Curves

1. Iron all fabrics.
2. For each color, cut the number of 2½" x WOF strips listed under First Cut in the **Cutting Chart: Curves**.
3. Subcut the strips into inner and outer curve pieces using the cumulus **2" outer quarter curve and inner quarter curve** templates on p. 38. Quantities are listed in the Second Cut section.
4. Combine the fabrics in the combinations shown in Piecing to make the curved block pieces.
   a. Following the combinations in the chart, take one outer curve piece and one inner curve piece. Fold each in half and finger press a crease in each at the spot shown in the diagram.
   b. Place the two pieces right sides together with the outer piece on top. Align the center crease and pin.

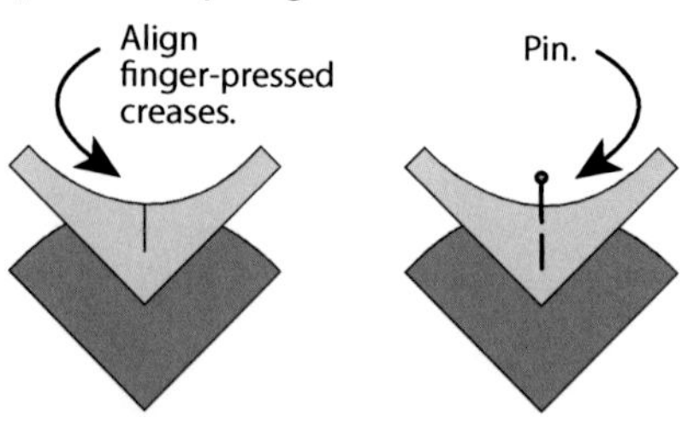

   c. Align the corners of the outer and inner curve pieces on the left side and pin. Repeat on the right side.
   Note: If you are unfamiliar with sewing curves, you may want to add more pins along the curve to hold the fabric in place while you sew.
   d. Keeping the outer curve piece on top, sew the curve with a ¼" seam. Press the seam towards the outer curve, making sure not to stretch the edges. The block will measure 2½" square.

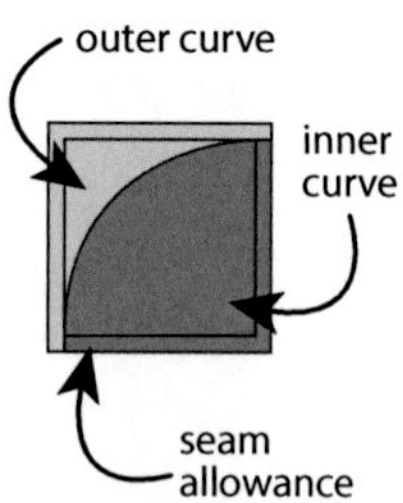

Curve Cutting Notes

- A 28mm rotary cutter can be helpful in cutting the tight curve of the outer quarter curve template.
- Be careful with the bias edges after cutting the curves. Starching before cutting can help keep the stretching under control.
- Don't try to cut too many layers of fabric at once. A sharp blade will cut accurate and smooth curves.

Step 3: Strip Assembly

Chain piecing is the simplest way to sew the strips. Normally I recommend assembling pixel-based quilts as Piece 1 to Piece 2, Piece 3 to Piece 4, Piece 5 to Piece 6, etc. However, this one works better using a different method. Each strip has an easily identifiable pattern of curves and rectangles/ squares. Sew each pattern group together, then those groups together into the finished strip.

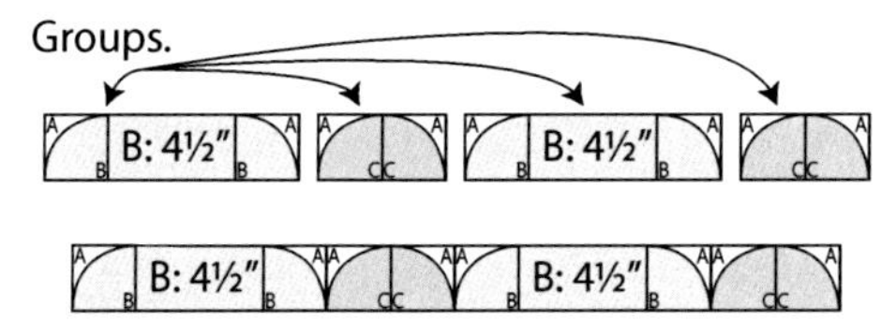

Note for making the King, Queen, Twin or Throw Quilts: The Quilt Assembly Diagram contains all five quilts, with bold lines showing the edges of each size. When piecing a quilt larger than Crib size, various pieces will be bisected along the smaller quilts' borders. Where two pieces of the same fabric meet across the border, you should combine those two diagram rectangles (noted in a bold italic type) and use a piece corresponding to the combined size (taking into account seam allowances). For instance, if constructing a Queen quilt, and the Twin quilt border divides two A pieces – A: 4½" and A: 4½", you should instead use a single A: 8½" piece. The Cutting Chart assumes you will make this substitution, and includes the larger combined pieces rather than the smaller divided pieces.

Because of the bisected strips, certain sized pieces will appear in the diagram even though they are not actually cut (ie, all the 6½" pieces). All of those pieces are matched with another piece of fabric to form a larger piece and that is the size cut and sewn.

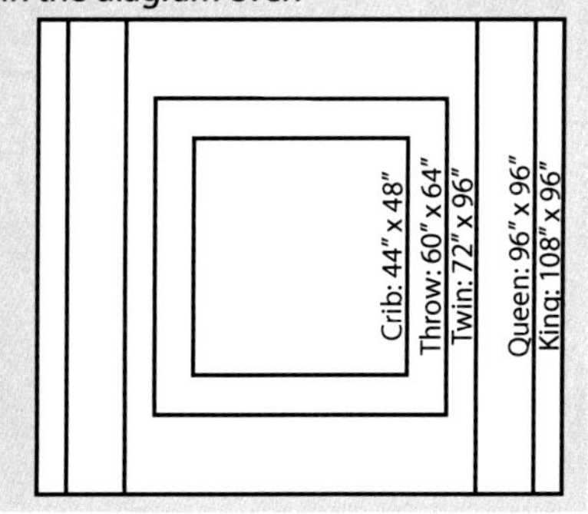

When sewing two quarter curve pieces together, make sure the seams at the top match.

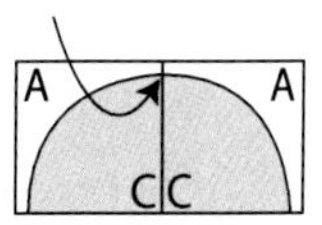

Set the strip aside until all the strips for that section are complete and then continue with **Step 4: Quilt Top Assembly**.

Strip Assembly Notes

- A ¼" seam allowance is used for all seams.
- Cut sizes are shown in the diagram.
- To help keep your place in the **Quilt Assembly Diagram**, use a blank piece of paper to underline the strip you are working on. Hold it in place with a small rotary cutting ruler or scissors.

Step 4: Quilt Top Assembly

1. When all the strips are complete, sew the strips together to form the quilt.
2. Press seams to one side.
   Note: It's best to wait until the entire quilt top is sewn together to press. With this many strips, distortion is inevitable so it's best for the strips in the quilt to become slightly distorted together.

Quilt Top Assembly Notes

- Do your best to sew accurate ¼" seams when sewing the rows so the quilt doesn't end up skewed.
- While a walking foot can help keep the strips aligned when sewing them together, it's not foolproof. Make sure to match up the seams as you sew the strips.

Step 5: Quilting and Finishing

1. Cut and piece your backing fabric.
2. Layer your backing, batting and quilt top. Baste.
3. Quilt, trim edges and add binding.

Quilting Idea

- Since these are clouds, quilt them as such. Think of a different design for each color and change threads as you move from the lighter clouds to the darker ones.

Cutting Chart: Rectangles and Squares

Size		A: White-1387	B: Silver-1333	C: Blue-1028	D: Shadow-457	E: Cloud-152	F: Baby Blue-1010	G: Ash-1007	H: Fog-444	I: Capri-442	J: Medium Grey-1223	K: Iron-408	L: Pewter-1470	M: Smoke-1713	N: Stratosphere-448	O: Shale-456	P: Oasis-446	Q: Graphite-295	R: Slate-1336	S: Steel-91	T: Celestial-233	U: Coal-1080	V: Prussian-454	W: Storm-458	X: Charcoal-1071	Y: Pepper-359
crib	**First Cut:** Number of 2½" x WOF rows to cut																									
crib								1	1	2	1	2	1	2	1	2	1	2	1	2						
crib	**Second Cut**																									
crib	8½"							3		6		6		6		6		6		3						
crib	4½"								8	3	8	3	8	3	8	3	8	3	8	3						
crib	2½"							2		4		4		4		4		4		2						
		A	B	C	D	E	F	G	H	I	J	K	L	M	N	O	P	Q	R	S	T	U	V	W	X	Y
throw	**First Cut:** Number of 2½" x WOF rows to cut																									
throw						2	2	3	2	3	2	3	2	3	2	3	2	3	2	3	2	2				
throw	**Second Cut**																									
throw	8½"					5		10		10		10		10		10		10		10		5				
throw	4½"						8	5	8	5	8	5	8	5	8	5	8	5	8	5	8	5				
throw	2½"						4		4		4		4		4		4		4		4					
		A	B	C	D	E	F	G	H	I	J	K	L	M	N	O	P	Q	R	S	T	U	V	W	X	Y
twin	**First Cut:** Number of 2½" x WOF rows to cut																									
twin		2	2	4	2	4	2	4	2	4	2	4	2	4	2	4	2	4	2	4	2	4	2	4	2	3
twin	**Second Cut**																									
twin	8½"	5		10		10		10		10		10		10		10		10		10		10		10		5
twin	4½"	2	12	9	12	9	12	9	12	9	12	9	12	9	12	9	12	9	12	9	12	9	12	9	12	7
twin	2½"			2		2		2		2		2		2		2		2		2		2		2		2
		A	B	C	D	E	F	G	H	I	J	K	L	M	N	O	P	Q	R	S	T	U	V	W	X	Y
queen	**First Cut:** Number of 2½" x WOF rows to cut																									
queen		2	2	5	2	5	2	5	2	5	2	5	2	5	2	5	2	5	2	5	2	5	2	5	2	3
queen	**Second Cut**																									
queen	8½"	7		14		14		14		14		14		14		14		14		14		14		14		7
queen	4½"	2	16	11	16	11	16	11	16	11	16	11	16	11	16	11	16	11	16	11	16	11	16	11	16	9
queen	2½"			2		2		2		2		2		2		2		2		2		2		2		2
		A	B	C	D	E	F	G	H	I	J	K	L	M	N	O	P	Q	R	S	T	U	V	W	X	Y
king	**First Cut:** Number of 2½" x WOF rows to cut																									
king		3	3	5	3	5	3	5	3	5	3	5	3	5	3	5	3	5	3	5	3	5	3	5	3	3
king	**Second Cut**																									
king	8½"	9		18		18		18		18		18		18		18		18		18		18		18		9
king	4½"		16	9	16	9	16	9	16	9	16	9	16	9	16	9	16	9	16	9	16	9	16	9	16	9
king	2½"		4		4		4		4		4		4		4		4		4		4		4		4	

Cutting Chart: Curves

		A: White-1387	B: Silver-1333	C: Blue-1028	D: Shadow-457	E: Cloud-152	F: Baby Blue-1010	G: Ash-1007	H: Fog-444	I: Capri-442	J: Medium Grey-1223	K: Iron-408	L: Pewter-1470	M: Smoke-1713	N: Stratosphere-448	O: Shale-456	P: Oasis-446	Q: Graphite-295	R: Slate-1336	S: Steel-91	T: Celestial-233	U: Coal-1080	V: Prussian-454	W: Storm-458	X: Charcoal-1071	Y: Pepper-359
First Cut: Cut the following number of 2½" x WOF rows.																										
crib								2	2	3	2	3	2	3	2	3	2	3	2	2						
throw						2	3	4	3	4	3	4	3	4	3	4	3	4	3	4	3	2				
twin		3	3	5	3	5	3	5	3	5	3	5	3	5	3	5	3	5	3	5	3	5	3	5	3	3
queen		3	4	6	4	6	4	6	4	6	4	6	4	6	4	6	4	6	4	6	4	6	4	6	4	3
king		4	5	7	5	7	5	7	5	7	5	7	5	7	5	7	5	7	5	7	5	7	5	7	5	4
Second Cut: Using the outer and inner curve templates, cut the following pieces from the 2½" strips.																										
crib	outer curve							22	16	22	16	22	16	22	16	22	16	22	16							
	inner curve								16	22	16	22	16	22	16	22	16	22	16	22						
throw	outer curve					30	20	30	20	30	20	30	20	30	20	30	20	30	20	30	20					
	inner curve						20	30	20	30	20	30	20	30	20	30	20	30	20	30	20	30				
twin	outer curve	36	24	36	24	36	24	36	24	36	24	36	24	36	24	36	24	36	24	36	24	36	24	36	24	
	inner curve		24	36	24	36	24	36	24	36	24	36	24	36	24	36	24	36	24	36	24	36	24	36	24	36
queen	outer curve	48	32	48	32	48	32	48	32	48	32	48	32	48	32	48	32	48	32	48	32	48	32	48	32	
	inner curve		32	48	32	48	32	48	32	48	32	48	32	48	32	48	32	48	32	48	32	48	32	48	32	48
king	outer curve	54	36	54	36	54	36	54	36	54	36	54	36	54	36	54	36	54	36	54	36	54	36	54	36	
	inner curve		36	54	36	54	36	54	36	54	36	54	36	54	36	54	36	54	36	54	36	54	36	54	36	54

Piecing: Make the following combinations using the curved piecing instructions in **Step 2: Cutting and Assembling Curves.**

outer curve	inner curve	crib	throw	twin	queen	king
A	B			24	32	36
A	C			12	16	18
B	C			24	32	36
C	D			24	32	36
C	E			12	16	18
D	E			24	32	36
E	F		20	24	32	36
E	G		10	12	16	18
F	G		20	24	32	36
G	H	16	20	24	32	36
G	I	6	10	12	16	18
H	I	16	20	24	32	36

outer curve	inner curve	crib	throw	twin	queen	king
I	J	16	20	24	32	36
I	K	6	10	12	16	18
J	K	16	20	24	32	36
K	L	16	20	24	32	36
K	M	6	10	12	16	18
L	M	16	20	24	32	36
M	N	16	20	24	32	36
M	O	6	10	12	16	18
N	O	16	20	24	32	36
O	P	16	20	24	32	36
O	Q	6	10	12	16	18
P	Q	16	20	24	32	36

outer curve	inner curve	crib	throw	twin	queen	king
Q	R	16	20	24	32	36
Q	S	6	10	12	16	18
R	S	16	20	24	32	36
S	T		20	24	32	36
S	U		10	12	16	18
T	U		20	24	32	36
U	V			24	32	36
U	W			12	16	18
V	W			24	32	36
W	X			24	32	36
W	Y			12	16	18
X	Y			24	32	36

Quilt Assembly Diagram

A When no width is given, use a 2½″ wide piece.

TEMPLATES

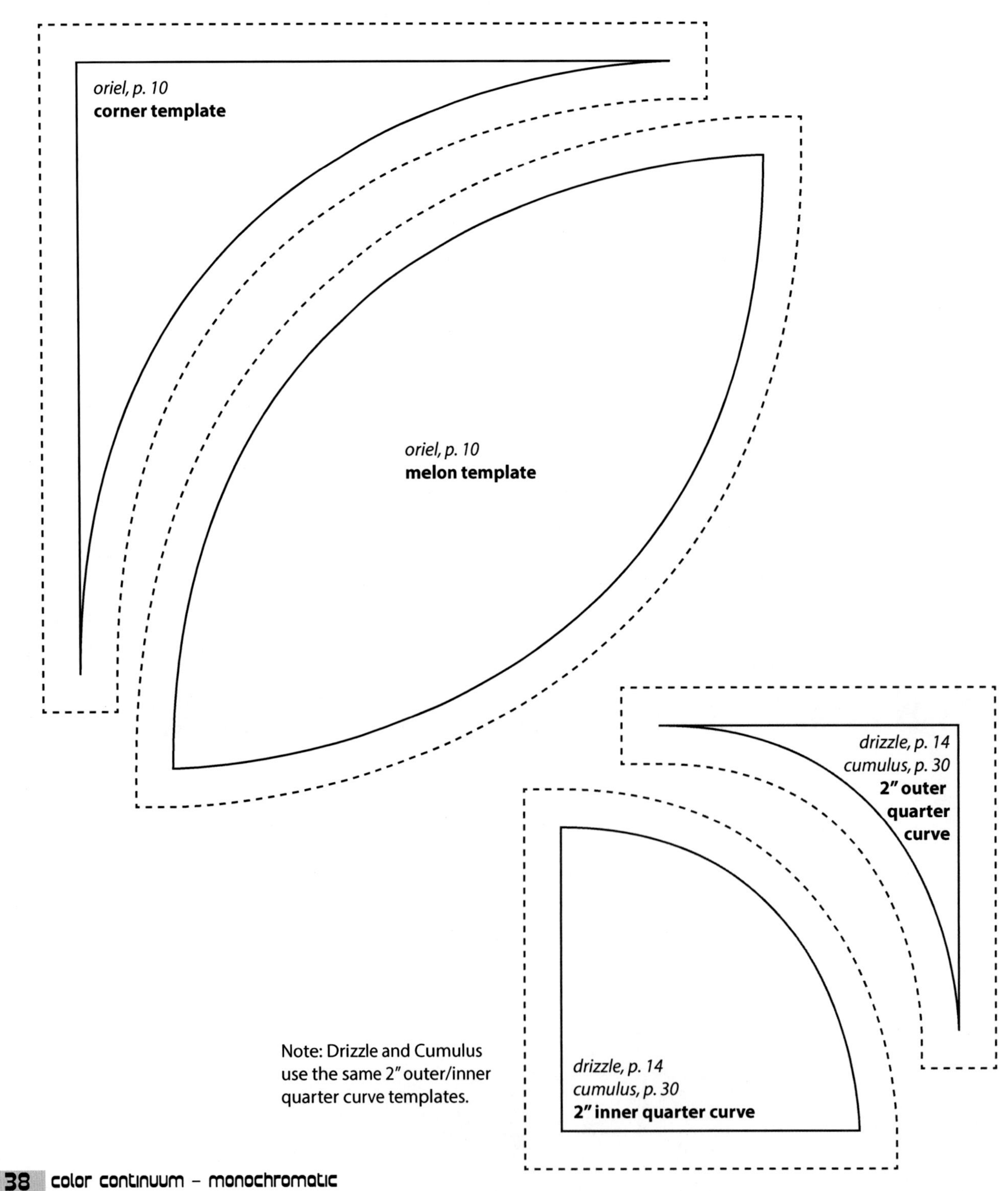

Note: Drizzle and Cumulus use the same 2" outer/inner quarter curve templates.

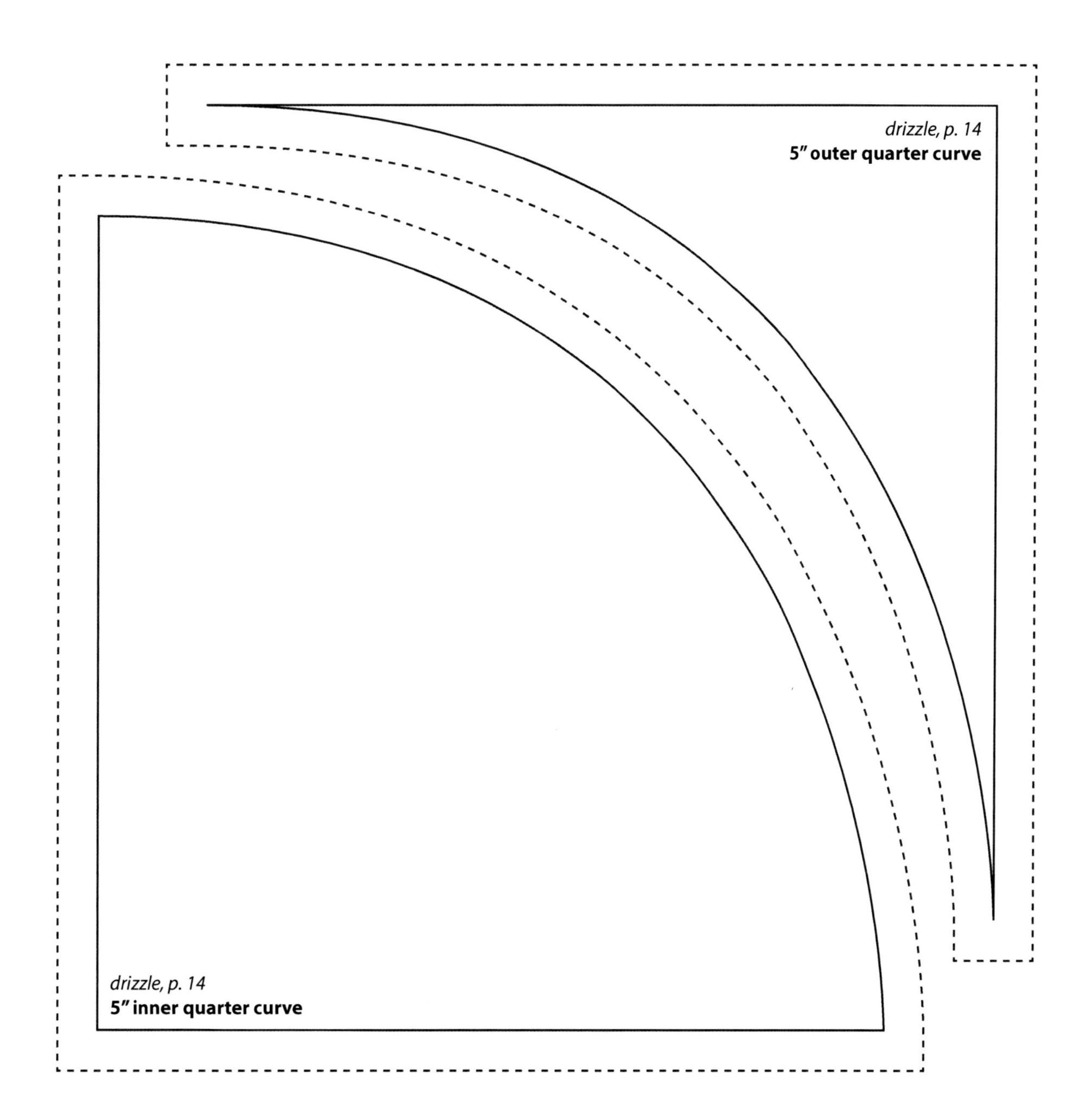
drizzle, p. 14
5″ outer quarter curve
drizzle, p. 14
5″ inner quarter curve

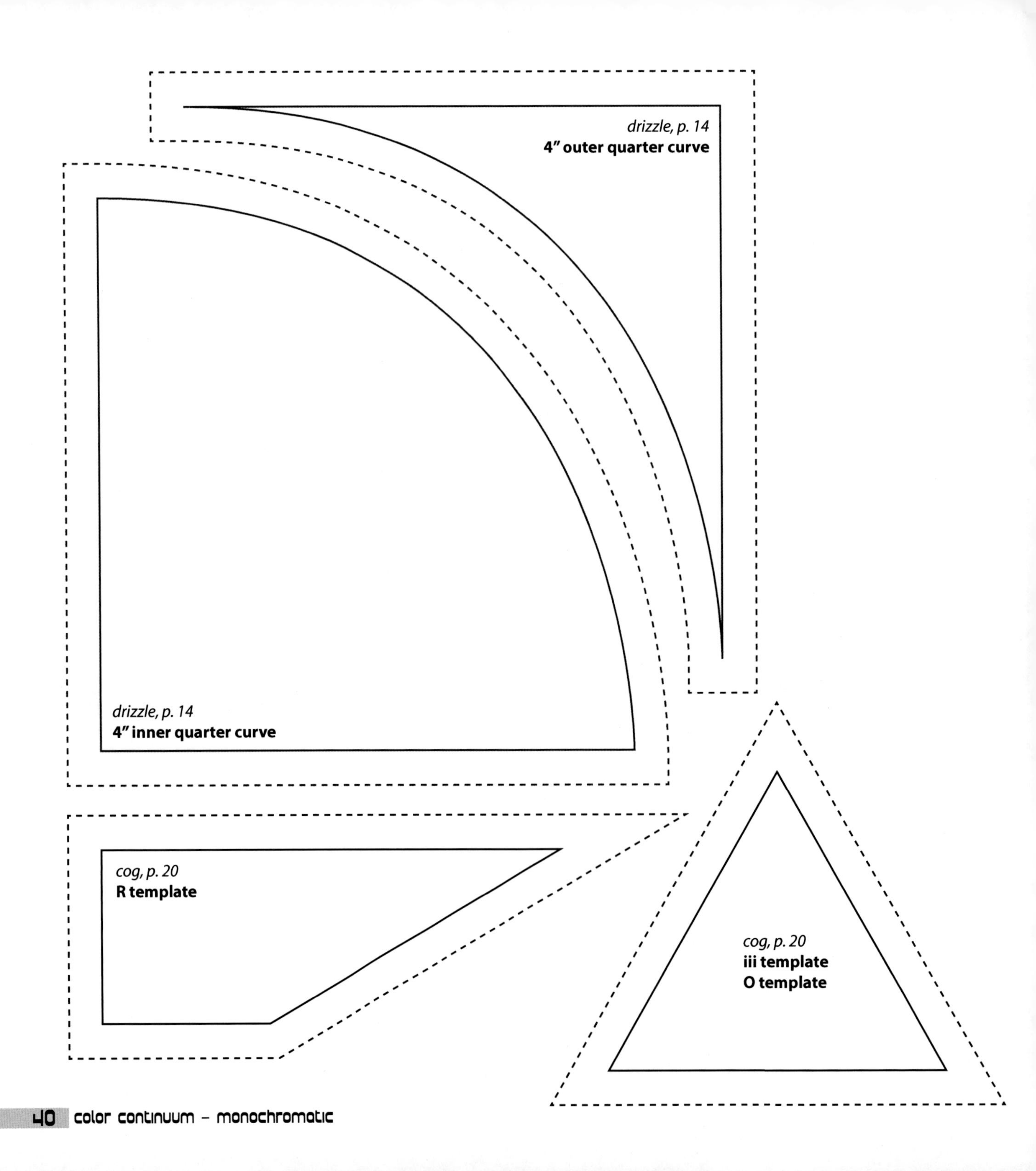

drizzle, p. 14
4" outer quarter curve
drizzle, p. 14
4" inner quarter curve
cog, p. 20
R template
cog, p. 20
iii template
O template

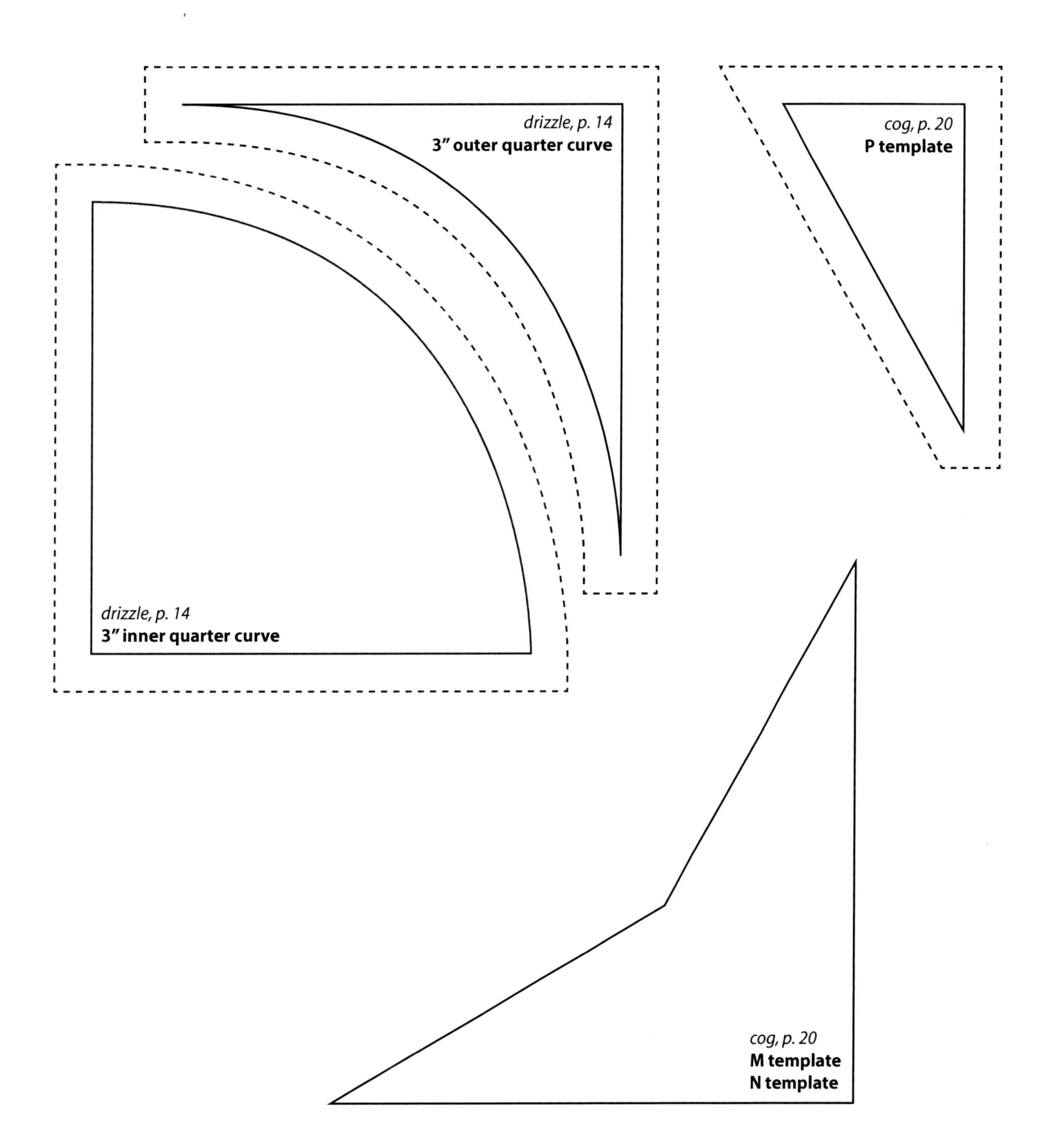
drizzle, p. 14
3" outer quarter curve
cog, p. 20
P template
drizzle, p. 14
3" inner quarter curve
cog, p. 20
M template
N template

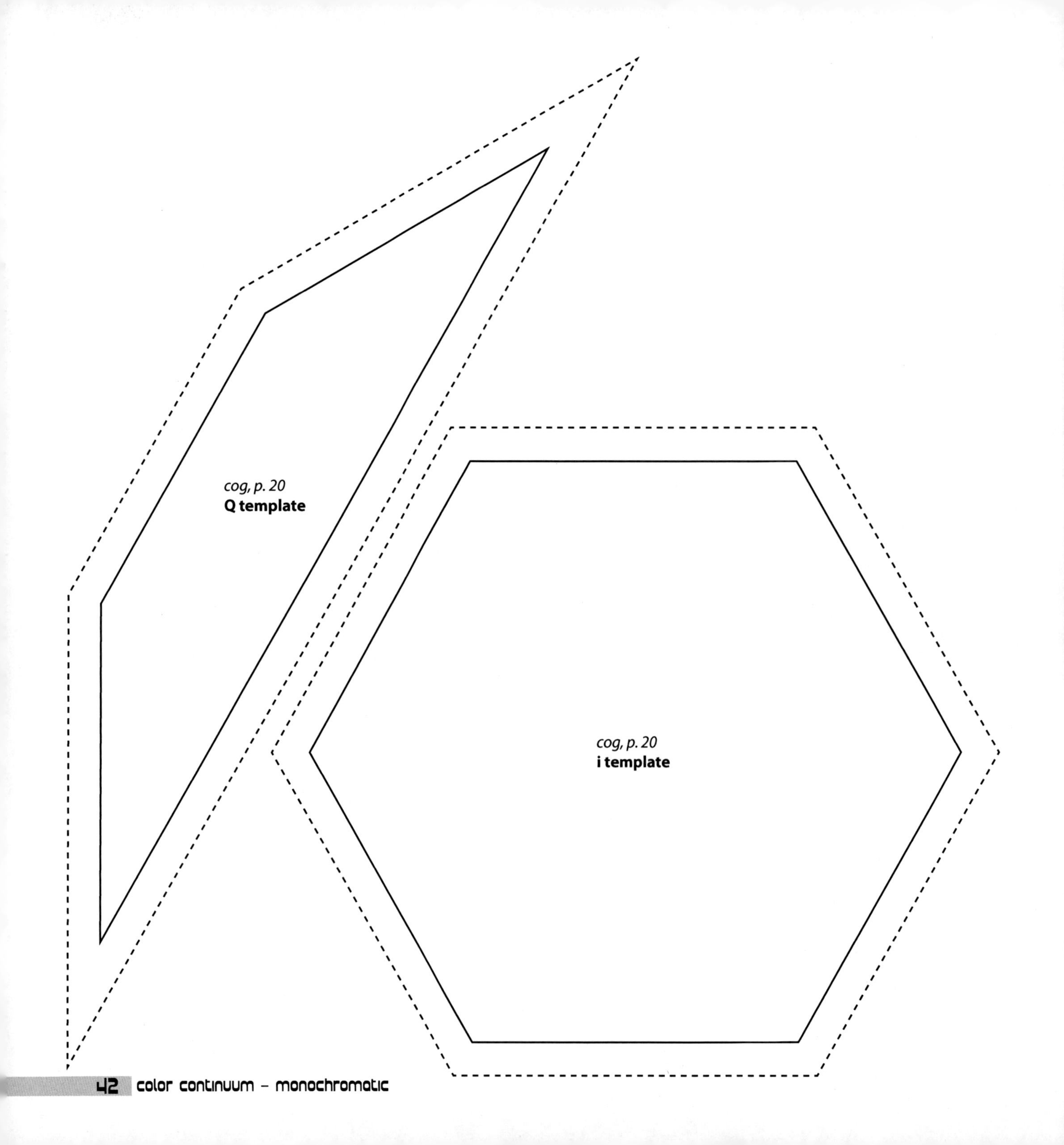

cog, p. 20
Q template
cog, p. 20
i template

resources

Kona Cotton Solids by Robert Kaufman Fabrics

Visit **robertkaufman.com** to see the complete Kona Cotton Solid range, purchase a color card and search for local and online fabric shops carrying Robert Kaufman fabrics.

Longarm Quilting by Angela Walters

Visit **quiltingismytherapy.com** for more information on Angela, her quilting, classes and books.

more from carolina patchworks

patterns

a variety of modern, bold quilt patterns available at **shop.carolinapatchworks.com**

available at
shop.carolinapatchworks.com
and **amazon.com**

Color, Block & Quilt gives a perspective on three different aspects of modern quilts — color schemes, block designs, and quilts — and then puts you in the driver's seat to come up with your own unique combination. Choose one of 15 different color schemes. Next, choose from 15 different modern block designs. Finally, pick a quilt design to serve as a framework for your creation, and fuse these elements together into a totally unique quilt project that's unlike anyone elses. 146 pages + cover

Architects need blueprints. Writers need drafts. Quilters crafting a creation from *Color Block & Quilt* need the *Workbook*. Well, you don't need it, strictly speaking, but it sure could help to have a paper models of the quilt you're going to make in order to get it just perfect before you put thread to fabric, couldn't it? 40 pages + cover

books

fabric

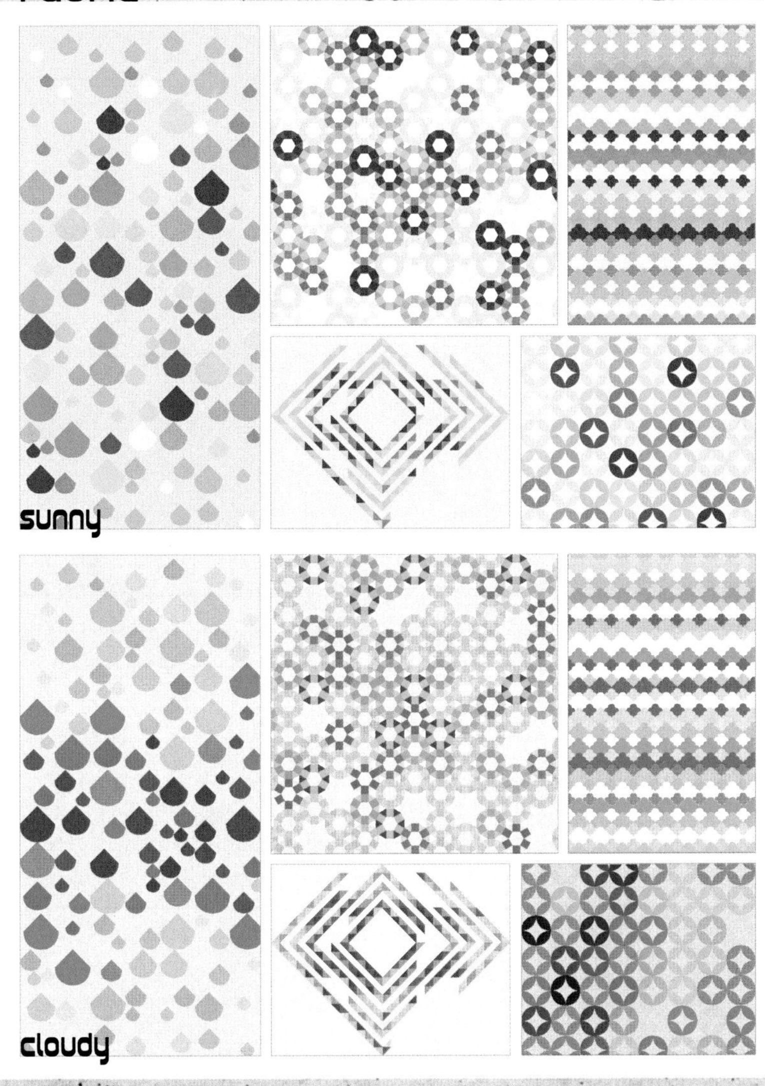

All of the quilts from **color continuum — monochromatic**, transformed into fabrics! In two (almost monochromatic) palettes: Cloudy and Sunny and are available in a variety of cuts and types of fabric.

available at
fabric.carolinapatchworks.com

about the author

Emily Cier desires only to live a normal life with her family in the Pacific Northwest. In order to achieve this goal, she must first rid herself of the plague of quilt designs, block ideas, shape concepts, and color palettes that invade her dreams, seep into her every waking hour, and deny her a moment's peace. Perhaps someday she will have satisfied the quilting spirits by translating all these ideas to concrete form. Until that day, she continues her daily toils to transcribe page after page of charts and illustrations.

Carolina Patchworks began as a way to fund Emily's fabric habit by selling the quilts she crafted, but has evolved over the years. Today, Carolina Patchworks has over 70 patterns in print, and including the tome you are holding in your hands, has penned five books on quilting. We can assure you, however, that there's more awesomeness yet to come.

For more of Emily's work, visit www.carolinapatchworks.com.

Made in the USA
Columbia, SC
09 August 2022